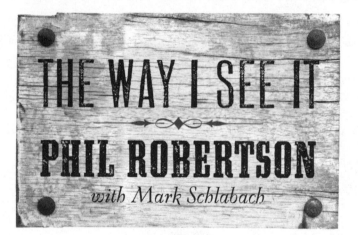

THE WAY I SEE IT

PHIL ROBERTSON

with *Mark Schlabach*

HOWARD BOOKS
A Division of Simon & Schuster, Inc.

NEW YORK   NASHVILLE   LONDON   TORONTO   SYDNEY   NEW DELHI

Howard Books
A Division of Simon & Schuster, Inc.
1230 Avenue of the Americas
New York, NY 10020

First Howard Books hardcover edition September 2014

HOWARD and colophon are trademarks of Simon & Schuster, Inc.

For information about special discounts for bulk purchases, please contact Simon & Schuster Special Sales at 1-866-506-1949 or business@simonandschuster.com.

The Simon & Schuster Speakers Bureau can bring authors to your live event. For more information or to book an event, contact the Simon & Schuster Speakers Bureau at 1-866-248-3049 or visit our website at www.simonspeakers.com.

Interior design by Jaime Putorti
Jacket design by Bruce Gore
Author photo © Russell A. Graves; all other images by Shutterstock

Manufactured in the United States of America

10   9   8   7   6   5   4   3   2

Library of Congress Cataloging-in-Publication Data

Robertson, Phil.
 UnPHILtered : the way I see it / Phil Robertson with Mark Schlabach.
   pages cm
1. Robertson, Phil. 2. Television personalities—United States—Biography. 3. Conduct of life. I. Schlabach, Mark, 1972- II. Title.
 PN1992.4.R535A3 2014
 791.4502'8092—dc23
 [B]
                     2014008730

ISBN 978-1-4767-6623-2
ISBN 978-1-4767-6624-9 (ebook)

To Miss Kay,

my best friend, who has been filtering

me to the outside world

for more than fifty years with her "Sarah spirit."

CONTENTS

CONTENTS

THE WAY I SEE IT

When I look back at the last forty or so years of my life, it's remarkable how much it has changed. About thirty years ago, I was fishing the Ouachita River near my home in Luna, Louisiana, earning thirty cents a pound on buffalo and seventy cents a pound on catfish. I was pulling in about $225 a week, which is how Miss Kay and I paid the bills and fed our four boys. Of course, the bulk of what we put on the table came from whatever game we shot in the woods and the fruits and vegetables that grew on our land.

Nowadays, because of the success of *Duck Dynasty*, they're telling my family that we won't ever have to work again. There's no doubt about it—the Almighty has blessed us immensely. Thirty years ago, all of my college buddies called me an idiot.

They told me I was squandering my college education by fishing the river and building duck calls. But I told them I knew it would work, and now they're calling me a genius!

I'm here to tell you that the American dream is still out there. My family and I are living examples of it. My company, Duck Commander, was a grassroots operation that started with nothing but the hopes and dreams of an entrepreneur. I built the company from scratch and didn't receive one penny from the U.S. government in turning it into a multimillion-dollar operation. I had a dream, and I stayed the course. I placed my trust in the Almighty and asked Him to bless my work. Then one day, I looked up, and it had worked out exactly like I'd prayed it would. I've been blessed, without question.

I'm living proof that here in America, you can start with nothing more than an idea and entrepreneurial spirit. If you provide the drive, dream, and vision, with God's help, you can accomplish anything.

But as you'll read in the pages that follow, I'm very concerned about the direction of our country. It looks nothing like the republic our founding fathers built more than two hundred years ago—or even like it did only a few decades ago. A large part of what was once the American culture is crumbling around us.

In this book, we'll tackle many of the most important and controversial issues facing America today—including abortion, gun control, government, politics, and race. As you might have guessed, I have some very strong opinions about the issues we face and will voice them in this book. But even more important to me than my opinions about America are my convictions about my faith. And I'm the first to admit that we Christians don't always express our political and social opinions in the kindest of spirits—I've been guilty of that myself in the past. In fact, some Christians give Christianity a bad name by the way they conduct themselves in the social arena. This is a real shame.

My utmost goal in life is to portray Christ as best as I can and share the Good News that He offers to each and every one of us. You might disagree with what I say or what side I'm taking on certain issues, but they're my opinions, and I try to share them in a kind way. And just as I believe I'm entitled to have opinions and speak out strongly about them, I believe that you have the right to have your opinions too, and I love you no matter where you stand on these issues. Let's show each other some respect and kindness as we express our opinions and beliefs.

> **But even more important to me than my opinions about America are my convictions about my faith.**

And here's where the undergirding spirit of this whole book comes into play: *love God; love your neighbor.* As I tackle some of the most controversial issues that face America, I believe the ultimate solution for all of them is found in these two powerful basics: *love God; love your neighbor.* If we all lived out those principles, I wouldn't need to write this book.

Please know that I never make any judgments about who's going to heaven and hell. That's the Almighty's job. My job is to love Him, love you, share the Good News, and then move on down the road.

I'm only an average man, and I'm confident there are people out there who are a lot smarter and more qualified than me. But in this book, I get to tell you what I believe and offer suggestions on how to turn our country around.

When I go out preaching and talking to groups across America, my main goal is to share my simple trust and faith in the death, burial, and resurrection of Jesus Christ. I want us to love God and love one another. That's it.

You might ask yourself, "You mean to tell me that's as profound as it's going to get?" Yep, that's all I'm trying to tell you, folks. It's not going to get any more complicated than that. Look, I don't have the brainpower, the know-how, or the inclination to go to Washington, DC, and try to fix our country. My purpose in life and in writing this book is only to point people to Jesus and to help turn our country's people around by reminding us all to love God and love one another.

For the life of me, I don't see the downside of human beings not being so mean to one another, not stealing from one another, and not murdering one another. We need to learn to forgive and love one another.

If, as a nation, we put the teachings of Jesus into practice, we'd be in a whole different place. Wouldn't we be better off being humble men and women? That's what Jesus told us to do. Wouldn't we be better off mourning with those who mourn, sharing their grief, and loving them dearly as neighbors, no matter their color? Wouldn't we be better off being meek, gentle, and kind—not given to violence? It would pretty much put an end to road rage, impatience, fighting, feuding, killing, and raping. Wouldn't we be better off trying to make peace instead of seemingly always being at war? Wouldn't we be better off as a society if we were merciful to the ones who are unfortunate? Wouldn't we be better off if there were a hunger and thirst inside all of us to do what's right? Wouldn't we be better off being pure in heart?

We all need to step back and take a look at our country. What do you see? Whether you're a believer or an unbeliever, a grandparent or a college student, a man or a woman, what do you see on our streets and in our schools? Be honest. Don't tell me you're not concerned by what's going on. Look around and listen. You might be asking yourself, "How in the world did people even come up with all of these harebrained ideas and ways to run a country?" I'm not saying I can fix it. What I'm saying is God can fix it when we live out those two simple principles: *love God and love one another.* When we remove God from the conversation—the only standard there is for morality, truth, law, and governing—what do we expect? When we remove the fear of God from any man or any movement, honesty, integrity, virtue, and morality leave with Him. They fly away and are gone.

My prayer is that by reading this book, maybe a few people

will come to trust in Jesus, turn from their sins, and grow closer to God. In the grand scheme of things, that's my biggest hope. That's my message in a nutshell: America, we have a love problem and we need to fix it. Let's try to love one another and see what happens. It can only get better.

PART ONE

PERSONAL LIFESTYLES

1

BIBLICAL CORRECTNESS

Fix No. 1: Replace Political Correctness
with Biblical Correctness

It will probably come as no surprise that there are a few people out there who wouldn't exactly describe me as "politically correct." My *Webster's Dictionary*, which was first developed by one of our founding fathers in the early nineteenth century—Noah Webster—defines being politically correct as "agreeing with the idea that people should be careful to not use language or behave in a way that could offend a particular group of people."

Hey, if what comes out of my mouth sometimes offends the people who don't believe what is written in the Bible, I'm guilty as charged. But understand this: I'm not trying to hurt anyone's feelings, and I don't dislike people simply because their opinions are different from mine. I don't hate anyone. In truth, I love everybody on this green earth. I don't believe in stereotypes, and I do believe in respecting everyone, regardless of whether they agree with my beliefs or not. All people, whether they're white, black, yellow, red, or green, are of great worth in God's eyes, and His desire for us all is that we share in His kingdom. Jesus actually *commanded* us to love. John 13:34–35 says, *"A new command I give you: Love one another. As I have loved you, so you must love one another. By this everyone will know that you are my disciples, if you love one another."*

I simply believe that what is written in the Scripture is the ultimate truth and that it's the blueprint for my life. I'm certainly not the first person to believe it. In the very first edition of *The American Dictionary of the English Language*, published in 1828, Webster wrote the following in the preface: "The moral principles and precepts contained in the Scriptures ought to form the basis of all our civil constitutions and laws. All the miseries and evils which men suffer from, vice, crime, ambition, injustice, oppression, slavery, and war, proceed from their despising or neglecting the precepts contained in the Bible."

> **I simply believe that what is written in the Scripture is the ultimate truth and that it's the blueprint for my life.**

It doesn't get much clearer than that, folks. Webster, who has been called the "father of American scholarship and education" and whose blue-backed speller books educated five generations of our country's children, spelled it out for us nearly two hundred years ago. Webster believed evil occurred because men and women neglected the Bible and didn't follow God's Word. We're still using Webster's dictionary today, so I guess he knew what he was doing. I imagine Mr. Webster is rolling in his grave now that words like *sexting, twerking,* and *selfie* are officially part of the English language. Hey, only in America, Jack!

Somewhere along the way, political correctness trumped biblical correctness in America, and in my opinion it's the cause of many of our country's problems today. Political correctness tries to dictate what is right and wrong, instead of our country having a moral system of righteous laws. Our society is overly sensitive, and we seem to be fixated on building up people's self-esteem and confidence. Hey, everybody needs constructive criticism once in a while. The way things are going, it's okay to have an opinion in America, as long as you don't offend anyone and don't quote the Bible. Many people today are eager to share the "positive" bits and pieces of the Bible in order to be politically correct but ignore the parts of the Scripture that might offend others.

In 2 Timothy 4:2–4, Paul the Apostle warned us of the consequences of being ashamed to preach the gospel, saying, *"Preach the word; be prepared in season and out of season; correct, rebuke and encourage—with great patience and careful instruction. For the time will come when people will not put up with sound doctrine. Instead, to suit their own desires, they will gather around them a great number of teachers to say what their itching ears want to hear. They will turn their ears away from the truth and turn aside to myths."*

I hate to tell you this, folks, but the times that Paul warned us about are here. Everywhere you look across our once-great land, politicians, special-interest groups, and people under the control of the Evil One are erasing any visible signs of Christianity. They're muzzling the people who speak the truth. If you speak out about sins like adultery, drunkenness, or sexual impurity, you're labeled as ignorant, insensitive, bigoted, or even hateful. The "PC police" constantly preach tolerance and acceptance, but they're intolerant of beliefs that aren't in line with their own. Certain Americans condemn businesses like Chick-fil-A for speaking out against same-sex marriages, but then we're told to celebrate companies like Ben & Jerry's ice cream and Starbucks because they embrace them. Is it not a two-way street? Isn't there supposed to be freedom of speech on both sides of the issue?

The amazing thing to me is that biblical correctness has never changed. It's written on the pages of the Bible and the words have remained the same through the ages. The sins are listed and are there for everyone to see. Each of us has the ability to read them, study them, and then decide whether we're going to sin or follow God's commands.

Conversely, political correctness is constantly changing and evolving. What might have been "PC" yesterday isn't "PC" today, even if it's only the smallest of things. Now, I'm all for being kind and thoughtful in the way we refer to people, but good grief! We get a bit ridiculous at times. Manholes have been renamed utility holes so as not to offend women, and blackboards are now called chalkboards so as not to offend African Americans. People who can't hear are no longer deaf; they're hearing impaired. People who can't see are no longer blind; they're visually impaired. People aren't even short anymore; they're vertically challenged. So do we call a bald man follically impaired? Political correctness is constantly morphing into a dark maze of nonsense. It keeps getting more and more nonsensical.

Yet, there has been a constant erosion of biblical correctness in our country. Look at the evidence in recent years:

■ A large cross that was prominently displayed outside a chapel at an isolated military base in northern Afghanistan was removed in 2011 because it didn't adhere to U.S. Army regulations. The army chaplain manual now prohibits permanent displays of religious symbols. I didn't serve in the military, but it would seem to me that the cross might be a source of comfort and relief to the troops who are risking their lives in battles in foreign lands. But, hey, that's just me.

■ In La Jolla, California, the American Civil Liberties Union and other groups are demanding that a twenty-nine-foot-tall cross that stands on government-owned land on Mount Soledad be dismantled. Crosses have been erected on the land since 1913, and the present cross is the centerpiece of a Korean War Memorial. The

ACLU contends the cross violates the separation of church and state because it demonstrates preference to a specific religion. In December 2013, a federal judge ordered the cross to be removed, but the case is being appealed.

■ At Camp Pendleton in California, U.S. Marines are fighting to keep two thirteen-foot crosses erected on a remote hill on the base. The memorial was first erected in 2003 by seven marines who were grieving for fallen soldiers lost in the war on terror. After the original cross was destroyed by a wildfire, a group of marines and widows carried two new ones up the hill. At the base of the crosses are several rocks, which were carried and left by the friends, widows, and children of fallen soldiers. A group called the Military Association of Atheists and Freethinkers is demanding that the crosses be removed. So far the marines haven't buckled, although a moratorium on the placement of religious symbols on bases has been put in place.

■ In 2012, the U.S. Forest Service denied an atheist group's request to have a Jesus statue removed from government-owned land on a Montana mountain. The statue was installed in 1955 by the local chapter of the Knights of Columbus as a memorial to local veterans of

World War II. Fortunately, the Forest Service extended the special-use permit for another ten years because the local community revered the statue and wanted it to stay.

The atheists and the other special-interest groups who are opposed to having crosses, statues of Jesus, and other religious symbols on public grounds say it's a matter of separation of church and state. But if you go back and read what our founding fathers said and wrote while they were building the greatest republic in the world, you would never conclude that they wanted to separate God from the fabric of political life in America. In fact, it's the last thing you would probably conclude. But now the thought police are trying to rewrite U.S. history. The men who signed the Declaration of Independence, like Benjamin Franklin, Samuel Adams, Benjamin Rush, and John Adams, were godly men. They were men who governed according to the principles of God and their conscience. But now we have men in power who have renounced the Bible, which is the only accurate map of the human heart that has ever been published.

> **The men who signed the Declaration of Independence were men who governed according to the principles of God and their conscience.**

There's evidence throughout American history that our government and its officials have often acknowledged God as the cornerstone of our laws and liberties. Don't believe me? Pull a few coins out of your pocket and read the inscriptions. "In God

We Trust" was first inscribed on U.S. coins in 1864 by an act of Congress, and in 1956 Congress made those sacred words our country's national motto. When George Washington became the first U.S. president in 1789 he added the words "so help me God" to his inauguration oath and many presidents since have spoken them. Since the early 1820s, the U.S. Supreme Court has opened its sessions with the prayer of "God save the United States and this Honorable Court," and Congress has started its sessions with prayer since 1789.

It wasn't only our founding fathers who were godly men. Many American presidents relied on their faith to guide them while serving in the most powerful position in the world. When children recite the Pledge of Allegiance before starting a school day—at least those who are still allowed to recite it—don't they say, "one nation under God, indivisible, with liberty and justice for all"? Do you know why? On June 14, 1954, President Dwight Eisenhower signed a bill into law that added "under God" to the Pledge of Allegiance. Eisenhower stated: "From this day forward, the millions of our school children will daily proclaim in every city and town, every village and rural school house, the dedication of our nation and our people to the Almighty. . . . In this way we are reaffirming the transcendence of religious faith in America's heritage and future; in this way we shall constantly strengthen those spiritual weapons which forever will be our country's most powerful resource, in peace or in war." President Eisenhower said our spiritual weapons would be America's most powerful resources, whether at peace or in war, and he was absolutely right. We need those resources more than ever in today's world.

During a speech before the Attorney General's Conference on Law Enforcement Problems on February 15, 1950, President Harry S. Truman said: "The fundamental basis of this nation's law was given to Moses on the Mount. The fundamental basis of our Bill of Rights comes from the teachings which we get from Exodus and St. Matthew, from Isaiah and St. Paul. I don't think we emphasize that enough these days." What would President Truman think about our country today?

Religion, the Bible, and the church are woven within the fabric of American heritage. There are religious symbols throughout Washington, DC. At the Supreme Court building, there's a marble frieze on the south wall of the courtroom that features Moses holding the Ten Commandments, along with images of Confucius, Muhammad, kings and various Greek philosophers. There is a statue of Moses in the rotunda of the Library of Congress, and the Ten Commandments are symbolized in the floor of the National Archives building. Even the Liberty Bell in Philadelphia, which is a symbol of American independence, was cast with part of the Scripture from Leviticus 25:10: *"Proclaim liberty throughout all the land unto all the inhabitants thereof."* Of course, many of those government buildings were constructed when faith and religion were still the foundation of our country. Are we going to one day remove these religious symbols from our history, too?

Nowadays, they're trying to remove the Ten Commandments from courtrooms across the country. In 2001, Roy Moore, then chief justice of the Alabama Supreme Court, installed a 5,280-pound granite monument of the Ten Commandments in the rotunda of the state's judicial building. Of course, it didn't take long for three attorneys to sue him, alleging that the monument was an unconstitutional state endorsement of religion. A U.S. district judge ordered Moore to remove the monument after he lost his appeal, and when Moore refused, he was removed from the bench by a state ethics panel.

In 2005, a sharply divided U.S. Supreme Court ordered that framed copies of the Ten Commandments on the walls of two rural Kentucky courthouses be taken down because they were violations of the separation of church and state. At the time, Justice Antonin Scalia, one of the dissenting voices, said the decision was inconsistent with our founding fathers' own views. In fact, Scalia recalled the dark day of September 11, 2001, when terrorists attacked New York and Washington, DC. When President George W. Bush spoke to the American people shortly after the attacks, he concluded his remarks with "God bless America." Scalia, who was in Rome that day, said a European judge confided that he wished more European leaders still included religious references in their speeches.

For the life of me, I can't figure out why anyone would want to remove the Ten Commandments from a courtroom. Let me get this right: you're an atheist and you're saying it's a violation of your rights to have to look upon the Ten Commandments when you walk into a courthouse. But much of the foundation of civil and criminal laws around the world was founded on the principles of the Ten Commandments. Okay, let's start with number five in the laws God gave to Moses on Mount Sinai. It says, *"Honor your father and your mother, so that you may live long in the land the Lord your God is giving you."* Well, let me ask you something: Where does law enforcement take your children when they find them drunk and tearing up other people's property? They take them to stand before a judge. If they honored their mothers and fathers, they wouldn't be disobedient and violate the laws of the land. Where do they take children when they really step out of line and are rebellious? They're going to take them to a juvenile court to determine their

> For the life of me, I can't figure out why anyone would want to remove the Ten Commandments from a courtroom.

punishment. It would seem to me that if the judge is going to try to teach a child a lesson for breaking the fifth commandment, the Ten Commandments might need to be hanging there for the child to see them.

If a man kills his neighbor, he has violated the sixth commandment, which says, *"You shall not murder."* If a judge is going to sentence him to life in prison, don't you think the Ten Commandments should be there so he can see what law he broke? If a man commits adultery and gets caught in the act by his wife, he has broken the seventh commandment, which says, *"You shall not commit adultery."* His spouse is probably going to take him to divorce court and take half of his money and possessions. And if a man gets caught robbing a bank, he has violated the eighth commandment, which says, *"You shall not steal."* The judge is probably going to sentence him to prison for knocking off the bank. Wouldn't that be a good time to read him the Ten Commandments?

What happened to our country, folks? Nowadays, our children no longer pray before the school day begins and greeters at certain department stores are no longer allowed to welcome customers with "Merry Christmas" during the holidays. In some schools, our children aren't even allowed to sing Christmas carols because the lyrics include "Christ." Don't even think about putting a nativity scene near a courthouse or public building! They might throw you in jail. When did Jesus Christ, the most perfect human to ever walk on the face of the earth, become a bad guy?

Political correctness trumps everything else in America nowadays, and I'm convinced it's another example of the Evil One's ploys to deceive us. Today's truth is based on what is socially acceptable, and biblical correctness has somehow become hate speech. Satan is a master deceiver, and he works to provide nonbelievers with a platform of acceptance. As it says in 2 Peter 2:2: *"Many will follow their depraved conduct and will bring the way of truth into disrepute."*

When you move Jesus out of the equation, all that's left is political wrangling. There's no Gospel, and there's no Good

News. So everyone tries to fix America's problems with politics alone—the spiritual realm has been pushed aside. America desperately needs a political correction that only God can give. Politicians can't fix the things that matter most, beginning with sin, physical death, righteousness, and holiness—we'll talk about these in the last section of the book. Attributes such as morality and integrity can't be legislated. Politics can't bring people peace, love, joy, honesty, and gentleness. Only following Jesus can do that.

Even though we're being scorned and mocked by the "PC police," we have to stand up for what we believe, regardless of the consequences. It's not about being politically correct; it's about being biblically correct. And with the direction America is headed, I'd much rather put my faith in the Bible than in politics. I'd rather our politicians be men and women who believe that the Bible is the Word of God. You want political correctness? Elect spiritual politicians who are biblically correct, and you will have it!

2

---◆◇◆---

SPIRITUAL DIETING

Fix No. 2: Count Your Sins, Not Your Calories

Oftentimes when I speak to a church congregation, sportsmen's club, or some other group around the country, I like to ask them one simple question. I look out at the audience and ask, "How many of you folks are over the age of ninety?" An older lady or man in the back of the room might raise her or his hand every once in a while, but it doesn't happen often, no matter where I am.

"What about all the calories you're counting?" I ask them. "What about all of the time you've spent on treadmills and bicycles? What about all that money you're spending on diets, gym memberships, and health food? What about all the weights you've lifted and the herbs and vitamins you've ingested? Even if you're doing all that, I doubt that many of us will make it to ninety."

According to recent studies, Americans spend north of $60 billion annually to try to lose weight and get themselves in better physical condition. Every week, 1.2 million people attend Weight Watchers meetings around the world, and more than 40 million Americans have a gym membership or own some sort of home exercise equipment. Each year, Americans spend about $18 billion on diet pills and appetite suppressants alone.

Americans are obsessed with losing weight and trying to live longer. I hate to break the news, folks: it's an exercise in futility. No matter what the diet gurus, nutrition experts, and health nuts tell you, American men are going to live to be about seventy-six years old. American women are going to live about five years longer, on average, but very few of us are going to reach age ninety, no matter how often we work out or how closely we watch our diets. Don't get me wrong, I don't think you should sit on the couch all day watching TV and eating potato chips and ice cream. That's the fastest and surest way to contract diabetes or suffer a heart attack or stroke. Go outside and get some exercise. Take a walk or ride a bicycle. Don't sit at the kitchen table and eat until you can't move. Use common sense. Enjoy your meals, eat until you're full, and then push your chair away from the table. Enough is enough. But that doesn't mean you should never enjoy fried chicken, fried catfish, banana pudding, peach cobbler, or the other foods that taste really good. Do you really want to spend the rest of your life consuming nothing but Brussels sprouts and tofu? Are we goats or humans? There has to be a middle ground, in which we can still eat the foods we enjoy while not struggling to fit through the door.

Somehow, counting calories became America's national pastime. Seemingly like clockwork, millions of Americans start every year on some sort of fad diet or health kick. You've probably done it a few times yourself. There was the cabbage soup diet, Israeli Army diet, South Beach Diet, Dr. Atkins's diet, Sugar Busters, and the Hollywood Diet. The people who came up with these diets became millionaires selling books and tasteless prepackaged foods, while the people who bought the products didn't lose anything on a long-term basis—except their minds! I can't believe someone hasn't already signed up Uncle Si to endorse a diet because the man can eat three helpings of fried squirrel and dumplings and not gain a single pound! He's so skinny he has to wear a belt with spandex! The man literally has to stand in the same place twice to cast a shadow. Talk about metabolism! For a man who does everything at a snail's pace and naps three times a day, Si's body must burn one hundred calories per minute. He's still as skinny as he was in high school.

> Do you really want to spend the rest of your life consuming nothing but Brussels sprouts and tofu? Are we goats or humans?

I'm not against diets or counting calories, but Americans are more concerned with physical fitness and what they eat than they are with their spiritual health. Look at the most popular New Year's resolutions for 2014, according to a survey by the University of Scranton in Pennsylvania: lose weight, get organized, spend less money and save more, stay fit and healthy, and quit smoking, among others. Wouldn't it be great if more people made New Year's resolutions to read the Bible more often or become closer to God? Believe me, the last thing you want to do is go on an extended spiritual diet—where you consume *nothing* of a spiritual nature. My spiritual diet lasted twenty-eight years, and the last four decades of my life have been a lot more enjoyable and fulfilling than the first three were.

Health care has become perhaps the biggest debate in America because it costs us so much money to stay alive. Obesity is a nationwide epidemic—about one-third of American adults are obese, according to the Centers for Disease Control and Prevention—and we're constantly being told to eat less and exercise more. Fair enough. But while we're focusing on counting calories and watching our carbohydrate and saturated fat intake, we'd better make sure our spiritual lives are being fed properly, too. Be careful what you take in, be careful what you partake of, and do everything in moderation. If you follow God's advice on living, don't you think you'll be more disciplined in your eating and exercise? Focusing on your spiritual well-being is what will give you eternal health care. In the end, physical dieting is still going to put you six feet underground—most of us long before we're ninety years old—no matter how hard you exercise or what you eat.

> Believe me, the last thing you want to do is go on an extended spiritual diet—where you consume *nothing* of a spiritual nature.

There's no question physical training is of some value while we're on this earth, but spiritual training is worth far more. In 1 Timothy 4:1–10, Paul the Apostle tells his younger protégé Timothy:

The Spirit clearly says that in later times some will abandon the faith and follow deceiving spirits and things taught by demons. Such teachings come through hypocritical liars, whose consciences have been seared as with a hot iron. They forbid people to marry and order them to abstain from certain foods, which God created to be received with thanksgiving by those who believe and who know the truth. For everything God created is good, and nothing is to be rejected if it is received with thanksgiving, because it is consecrated by the word of God and prayer.

If you point these things out to the brothers and sisters, you will be a good minister of Christ Jesus, nourished on the truths of the faith and of the good teaching that you have followed. Have nothing to do with godless myths and old wives' tales; rather, train yourself to be godly. For physical training is of some value, but godliness has value for all things, holding promise for both the present life and the life to come. This is a trustworthy saying that deserves full acceptance. That is why we labor and strive, because we have put our hope in the living God, who is the Savior of all people, and especially of those who believe.

After you've read the Scripture, what do you think you should be majoring in while you're down here on earth—physical training or spiritual training? You might want to focus on your spiritual training because you'll be much better off. Spiritual training not only holds promise, but it also gives you peace of mind while you're living on earth. Riding a stationary bike or running on a treadmill is only going to get you so far. You might shed a few pounds, and it might be easier to fit into your favorite blue jeans, but that's about as far as exercise is going to get you. Sure, it might add five or ten years to your life, but I want to live forever—eternally!

It's a good thing to keep your body in decent physical shape, but don't be telling others they can't eat this or that. America has gone overboard with dieting and exercise. Don't be fooled—the people who are running marathons and triathlons are dying like everybody else. As far as I'm concerned, the passage gives us permission from headquarters to eat what we desire, despite what the vegans, vegetarians, and animal rights activists would lead us to believe. God said everything He *"created is good, and nothing is to be rejected if it is received with thanksgiving"* (1 Timothy 4:4). The Bible doesn't say anything about not shooting and eating ducks, deer, rabbits, or squirrels. Hey, I almost feel bad for the animals, but they either need to run faster or quit tasting so good!

Believe me, being spiritually flabby is far worse than being a little plump physically. When you think of a balanced diet, I'm sure what you're eating pops into your head. Nutritionists make recommendations for how much calcium, fat, fiber, and protein we're supposed to eat each day and how many carbohydrates, vitamins, and minerals. They tell us what we're supposed to eat and what we're not supposed to eat. But a true balanced diet involves much more than only what we're putting in our stomachs. Our bodies consist of the spirit and flesh. We can't function properly if we're feeding only one part and neglecting the other. Satan wants us to focus on the flesh because he knows our spirit is what is connected to God. Therefore we need to develop our spirits as much as we nurture our bodies.

Being spiritually flabby is far worse than being a little plump physically.

In the few verses below, Paul the Apostle laid out an entire set of ground rules for spiritual well-being:

You were taught, with regard to your former way of life, to put off your old self, which is being corrupted by its deceitful desires; to be made new in the attitude of your minds; and to put on the new self, created to be like God in true righteousness and holiness.

Therefore each of you must put off falsehood and speak truthfully to your neighbor, for we are all members of one body. "In your anger do not sin": Do not let the sun go down while you are still angry, and do not give the devil a foothold. Anyone who has been stealing must steal no longer, but must work, doing something useful with their own hands, that they may have something to share with those in need.

Do not let any unwholesome talk come out of your mouths, but only what is helpful for building others up according to their needs, that it may benefit those who listen. And do not grieve the Holy Spirit of God, with whom you were sealed for the day of redemption. Get rid of all bitterness, rage and anger, brawling and slander, along with every form of malice. Be kind and compassionate to one another, forgiving each other, just as in Christ God forgave you. (Ephesians 4:22–32)

How do you become more spiritually fit? For starters, this passage talks about putting off your old self and becoming new. You've seen those before-and-after pictures of people who supposedly have followed some diet plan and lost tons of weight—they look like new people. Well, God is calling us to become new on the inside.

When we are baptized into Christ, our former self is buried. The old man is gone, and the new re-created man is to be like God in true righteousness and holiness. Where do we start in this re-creation? Read the Scripture: *"Put off falsehood and speak truthfully to your neighbor, for we are all members of one body."* Quit lying and speak the truth. We have to remember that people will not always like it when we tell the truth, especially if we say things they don't want to hear. But it is important to speak the truth, no matter what others want you to say. God doesn't like it when we lie.

Then the Scripture says: *"In your anger do not sin."* Anger itself is not a sin; there are some things we should be angry about. If six thugs beat up an elderly woman and steal her purse, we should be angry about it. If a con man takes advantage of us, we should be mad about it. It isn't right. But you don't have to sin when you're upset. If you get angry with your wife during an argument, you might want to start cursing her. You're sinning. If you're so mad at her that you lash out and hit her, you've sinned big-time. What's the way out? Turn and walk away and don't say a word. But if you walk away and you're still bitter and angry and won't turn it loose, you're still sinning. The only way you're going to get out of it without sinning is to forgive her, don't hold it against her, and go on down the road.

If you've been a thief or a burglar, quit stealing and go to work. Instead of taking things from others, do something useful with your hands so you'll be able to share it with somebody in need.

And hey, how hard would it be to get that filthy language out of your mouth? Only say things that help build people up and get the negative, unwholesome, filthy, vile language out of your mouth.

Paul goes on to tell us to get rid of bitterness, rage, anger, brawling, and slander and be kind and compassionate to others. We need to imitate God and live a life of love.

We must learn how to forgive each other and not hold grudges. In the Ephesians passage, Paul the Apostle tells us: *"Do not let the sun go down while you are still angry."* Don't become bitter, because the sun will go down and you'll still be mad. Some people hold grudges for years and it isn't healthy. If you stay mad more than a day, you're giving the devil a foothold. We need to have mercy and forgive each other, as God is merciful in forgiving us.

Hey, if someone is trying to steal something from you, let him have it. It's like the time I caught the men stealing fish from my nets in the Ouachita River when I was still a commercial fisherman. Even after I caught them red-handed, I told them they could keep the fish. Of course, they looked at me like I was half nuts (I was holding a shotgun in my lap), but they never came back and stole from me again.

If people get mad at you, don't retaliate. If somebody insults you, what are you going to do? Nothing—except love them. Who is the stronger man? The man who gets insulted and wants to fight, lashing out with his tongue, fists, or a gun, or the man who forgives, walks away, and doesn't hold it against him? Remaining silent while being insulted is wise. That's the difference between being a spiritual man and being an ungodly man. Nowadays, people want to fight over anything, even the most trivial of matters. But spiritual people say, "Hey, I don't hold it against you, brother. No problem." A weak man retaliates quickly; a strong man is slow to anger. If the other person lashes out at you, tell them, "Hey, I still love you." It's really that easy.

> Who is the stronger man? The man who wants to fight or the man who forgives and walks away?

We must also learn to have forgiveness in our hearts. God has forgiven all of our sins and we need to readily forgive others, too. You might ask: How many times do I have to forgive them,

Phil? Seven times, maybe? Jesus said "seventy times seven." You have sinned more than seven times, have you not? Do what He said—seventy times seven or forever!

Basically, spiritual training is this: you take away the bad and replace it with good. After my romping and stomping days, I was converted and baptized. I put my former life in the rearview mirror and was born again. I ran with the wicked for twenty-eight years. The last thirty-nine years, I've run with the Jesus people. The contrast is astounding; it's like night and day. I asked the man who converted me, "Hey, let me ask you something. How long does it take to get these wicked thoughts out of my mind?"

"Phil, how long did it take you to put them there?" he asked me.

"Twenty-eight years," I told him.

"Well, it will be a while," he said. "Think of your biblical heart as a computer. You put material into your heart like you do when you load information into a computer. What you put into your heart is what is eventually going to come out of your mouth."

Much like dieting, achieving spiritual well-being takes time and discipline. Unfortunately, we live in a society that seems to want to offer a quick fix for every one of our problems. There are one-day seminars or audio courses for everything—as long as we're willing to pay the price. We can learn Spanish, French, or some other foreign language in four weeks or less by listening to audio lessons. We can learn to play the guitar in only a few short weeks; you can even become a "pastor" with a few clicks on your computer. Too many people aren't willing to put in the time and practice to master skills anymore.

But the bottom line is you will not lose weight if you're not disciplined about your diet and exercise. Likewise, you will not succeed spiritually if you do not become a disciplined person and put in the necessary time and effort. Discipline requires motivation, and there's no greater motivation than eternity. Pray to God and read the Bible. You have to *want* to lose weight, and you have to *want* to become a better Christian and person. 1 Peter 2:1–3 tells us, *"Therefore, rid yourselves of all malice and all deceit, hypocrisy, envy, and slander of every kind. Like newborn babies, crave pure spiritual milk, so that by it you may grow up in your salvation, now that you have tasted that the Lord is good."*

Instead of growing in our faith, too many of us are content to remain infants. We should be eating solid foods, not milk, but we are unwilling to develop and mature. In order to grow, we need to deepen our faith and understanding of His word. Rather than obsessing about our diets, cholesterol, and calories, we should give much more energy to investing in eternal health care, the grace of God given through Jesus. Hope is a wonderful thing, and I don't see any hope outside of Jesus. Peace with God is hope.

So take care of your spiritual well-being, and eat all the fried chicken and pecan pie you want.

3

———◆———

MONEY

Fix No. 3: Focus on Your Eternal Inheritance, Not Your Portfolio

People ask me all the time how the success of *Duck Dynasty* has changed my life. Well, I can't go many places without being noticed anymore. But it was kind of that way before the TV show came along. Hey, I'm pretty hard to miss because of my beard and camouflage clothes! I've noticed that I usually have a much bigger audience when I go speak at churches and other groups, and, of course, Miss Kay and I have a little more money in the bank.

Is it more fun being rich than poor? Sure, it's a lot more fun having money in the bank, instead of having to worry about how you're going to pay your bills every month. I guess having money in the bank gives you a little bit of peace of mind, but it really hasn't changed our lifestyle very much. When I was fishing the Ouachita River for a living, I made about $225 a week. I had to break my back every day to earn the money. It was hard work, but I never complained. Even though we didn't have much in terms of money and material possessions, the Robertsons were a happy family. We managed to make do with what we had, which wasn't much, and I don't think my boys ever felt like they were missing out on anything. We always had enough bait, ammunition, and patience to catch or shoot what we needed to eat, and Miss Kay and my parents grew plenty of fruits and vegetables in our garden. I took ol' Ben Franklin at his word: "He that waits upon fortune, is never sure of a dinner."

We're certainly eating a lot better now than we were before. Instead of having crappie, catfish, duck, or crawfish seven days a week, we'll eat a rib-eye steak or lobster every now and then. But we're still eating a lot of duck and crawfish—our appetite for those delicious foods will never change. We're living in the same house we purchased in 1976, and I'm still driving a pickup truck. I guess some things will always stay the same. However, I have noticed a few big changes since the money came rolling in. Miss Kay had bigger closets built in our bedroom because our stuff was piled up in a little tight space. We have a pretty small house; there's a kitchen, dining area, living room, two bedrooms, and two bathrooms. It's nice to have a bigger closet to hold more camouflage clothes, guns, and ammo for duck season. She also added a bigger pantry in the kitchen to store more canned goods, such as mayhaw jelly, chowchow, and pickled vegetables.

Miss Kay recently had an outdoor country kitchen built next to our house so she would have a bigger space to cook when we entertain family, friends, and other guests. It has a bigger stove that makes it easier for her to cook, and it doesn't get so hot in the kitchen during the summertime when she's frying fish and preparing other dishes. We have more grub, more camouflage clothes, and more shoes for Miss Kay. I guess those are the first things rednecks buy when the money starts coming in.

Now, I have to admit that I have expanded our duck hole a little bit. I purchased an additional twenty acres on one side of my property and about forty-five acres down the way. We were trying to make our duck hole a little more productive, and now there is additional land to plant more corn and other crops to try to attract more ducks. My sons will inherit my land when I die, so it will give them a place to hunt with their kids, grandkids, and great-grandkids. It will pay off in the future for my sons, and the property will stay within the Robertson family. I'm leaving them a good inheritance.

But more important, I'm thinking about the inheritance my family will have in the afterlife. Romans 8:14–17 tells us: *"For those who are led by the Spirit of God are the children of God. The Spirit you received does not make you slaves, so that you live in fear again; rather, the Spirit you received brought about your adoption to sonship. And by him we cry, 'Abba, Father.' The Spirit himself testifies with our spirit that we are God's children. Now if we are children, then we are heirs—heirs of God and co-heirs with Christ,*

*if indeed we share in his sufferings in order that we may also share
in his glory."*

You have to understand this: God adopts people who come
to Jesus. When you come to Jesus, you're born of God. You
are free from sin and death because Jesus paid for your sins on
the cross and because God accepted His sacrifice. Once you're
born of God, He becomes your Father. You end up inheriting what your Father has. It's like what my four sons and
their families will inherit from me when I'm six feet under the
ground on the physical earth. The Spirit Himself, the Holy
Spirit, frees us and gives us the power to really live for God.
Once you're sealed with the Spirit, it means you're God's child.
Now, the Bible tells us that if we're His children, then we're His
heirs and co-heirs with Christ: *"Now if we are children, then we
are heirs—heirs of God and* co-heirs *with Christ, if indeed we
share in his sufferings in order that we may also share in his glory"*
(emphasis added). So, yes, God's children have an inheritance
coming. We're adopted and added to God's family, and Jesus is
our brother, our savior, and our Lord. As co-heirs with Jesus,
we get what His father has. How could you ever want anything
more?

The U.S. economy is in terrible shape, and it has been that
way for the last six years. Americans are worried about the bal-
ances of their bank accounts and retirement savings. They're
concerned about the stock market, interest rates, and inflation.
They're worried about the rising costs of health care and the

declining values of their homes. But as children of God, our focus needs to be on spiritual things, and we need to quit worrying so much about financial things.

Money is fleeting. It is here today and gone tomorrow. True financial success and happiness come not from accumulating a big balance in your checking account but from following God's plan for your life. He will provide for all of your needs. If you put your faith in Jesus and know that you will ultimately inherit what God has, you'll be content with what you have while you're on earth. If the riches come, so be it. Be generous with what you have and help care for your neighbors, the sick, and the poor. But you need to remember this: at the end

> If you end up inheriting what the Creator of the cosmos has, you will have everything there is, because God owns it all.

of the day, if you end up inheriting what the Creator of the cosmos has, you will have everything there is, because God owns it all. What a thought! You'll want for nothing. That is the promise God made to us—we will inherit everything He has made. Talk about inheriting some land!

I can honestly say that I never contemplated getting rich, even after Duck Commander took off and *Duck Dynasty* started getting bigger and bigger. I was perfectly content making $225 a week fishing the river and selling a few thousand duck calls every year. I was able to make a living doing what I loved to do most, and that's hunting ducks and fishing the river. I think that's why so many people tell me that I'm the same way now that I was when I didn't have much. I was and am perfectly happy, as long as I'm doing what I love.

I truly believe there's a difference between getting rich and God blessing you mightily. The love of money and the never-ending quest to make it are the roots of all kinds of evil. Sadly, when the stock market collapsed, we had stockbrokers jumping out of windows to their deaths. Children are killing each other over expensive tennis shoes. The bankruptcy and foreclosure statistics in America are staggering. People are spending money beyond their means because they're trying to keep up with the Joneses. It's nonsense.

America's quest for money is rampant. We've become consumed by material possessions, wanting what others have and trying to build our bank accounts as big as we can. Coveting—or wanting—what our neighbors have is a sin. God's blessings for them may not be His blessing for us.

When I think about America's thirst for money and material possessions, I recall a story told to me in church one Sunday not too long ago. Although I'm not entirely sure the story is factually accurate, I think it gets my point across. In 1923, eight of the wealthiest men in America met at the Edgewater Beach Hotel in Chicago. The group included the head of one of the world's greatest monopolies, one of the most successful speculators on Wall Street, a former president of the largest U.S. steel company, a past chairman of one of the country's largest utility companies, a past president of the New York Stock Exchange, a future president of the Bank for International Settlements, and a past member of U.S. president Warren G. Harding's cabinet. Together, the men were worth billions of dollars and controlled more money than the U.S. Treasury did at the time.

Well, money certainly didn't buy the multimillionaires happiness. Ivar Kreuger, who built a global matchbook empire, committed suicide. Jesse Livermore, who was known as the "Great Bear of Wall Street" and was famous for building and then losing several multimillion-dollar fortunes during the stock market crashes of 1907 and 1929, killed himself in the cloakroom of a New York hotel. Leon Fraser, head of the Bank for International Settlements, also committed suicide. Charles M. Schwab, the American steel magnate, died a pauper after blowing through a fortune that would have been worth an estimated five hundred million to eight hundred million dollars today. Samuel Insull, chairman of Commonwealth Edison Company, was acquitted of bilking investors and died of a heart attack after losing most of his fortune. The other three men—Associated Gas and Electric Utility president Howard Hopson, New York Stock Exchange president Richard Whitney, and former U.S. secretary of the interior Albert Fall—served prison sentences before their deaths.

That story reminds me that money and power won't bring you happiness. There are plenty of modern-day examples of millionaires and billionaires blowing through their fortunes through lavish spending and irresponsible stewardship. We see it over and over again in Hollywood and professional sports.

When an actor or athlete reaches the pinnacle of his or her profession, they sign multimillion-dollar contracts and don't know how to handle their newly found fortunes. They surround themselves with big entourages, and their family members and greedy friends can't wait to get their hands on the money. They don't have a lot of discipline in their lives, there's no Jesus, and so they spend millions of dollars in a matter of months. When the dust settles, their money is gone and their friends are nowhere to be found. They burn out and end up broke and destitute. They are left thinking, *What in the world happened?* Well, they were caught up in the rat race of extravagant living and didn't make sound decisions about their lives. Like I said, money can be here today and gone tomorrow.

The truth is that God owns everything and everything we receive comes from Him. God is the one who created all the earth, and all in it belongs to Him. We might have to work hard to earn a living, but God is the one who gives us the health and strength to complete our jobs. We shouldn't strive to be rich, and as Christians we shouldn't hoard our money. Our goal should be to live below our means and be content with what God has given us. There's a big difference between necessities and desires, and we need to stop buying indulgences only because we have the available credit to purchase them. God doesn't want us to go into debt. Instead, we should save money for unforeseen expenses and emergencies and give generously to the church and other charitable organizations. Our hearts should always be on the lookout for how we can help the people who need it most.

Managing your money isn't hard. Before you buy something, whether it's a new TV, truck, gun, or shirt, ask yourself one question: "Do I really need it?" Is it a necessity or is it a luxury? Before I became semifamous and car dealers started giving me trucks to drive, I drove them until the wheels fell off. Even though clothing companies like Under Armour now give me whatever I want to wear, I still wear my socks and T-shirts until they can't be worn anymore. When you flip on your TV, do you really need three hundred channels? Do you think you could get by with only sixty? Look around your house, and I'm sure you'll find dozens of ways to save money if you really think about it. I can tell you this: you'll rarely see me eating out in a restaurant. I don't understand why so many Americans want to eat their meals at fast-food joints or fancier sit-down restaurants. It's going to cost you twice as much to eat, and it's not going to taste nearly as good as what you could cook at home. Why would you want to eat your meals in a restaurant full of strangers instead of eating a home-cooked meal with your loved ones at the dinner table? Americans spend about forty-five billion dollars a month eating out, according to research from the U.S. Census Bureau, and sales at eating and drinking places have reached an all-time high!

When is America going to learn that money won't solve all of its ills? First Timothy 6:6–7 says: *"Godliness with contentment is great gain. For we brought nothing into the world, and we can take nothing out of it."* You can amass a fortune while you're on earth, but trust me, dude, you're not taking any of it with you. Where you're going it wouldn't make any difference, so quit running so fast and trying to amass money. Learn the secret of godliness with contentment. It's not about money, no matter how much you make. When you die, they're going to put your best duds on you and then others are going to fight over what you amassed.

> You can amass a fortune while you're on earth, but trust me, dude, you're not taking any of it with you.

Once you're in the ground, they'll haggle over your cash, house, cars, guns, and boats. You're not taking any of it with you. When certain funeral homes are asked to provide clothing for the deceased, the undertakers purposely dress men in suits without pockets. Hey, there aren't any pockets because you're not taking anything with you!

When Miss Kay and I decided to slow down and have less of a role at Duck Commander, we all but gave the company to our sons. Duck Commander certainly wasn't what it is today, but it was successful enough for my three sons to make a pretty good living. Willie had the best business mind out of the bunch. Even when he was in junior high, he was bootlegging candy and all but took over the concession business. The principal called me and chewed me out about it.

We designated Willie to be the CEO of Duck Commander, and he and his wife, Korie, ended up buying the company from us. The rest of my sons also work for Duck Commander. My oldest son, Alan, who is a preacher, is the spiritual adviser of the bunch. Jase is the best hunter among the boys and probably has the most analytical mind. He makes sure the duck calls are built correctly and sound exactly like ducks. Jep, my youngest son, shoots and edits our video for our hunting DVDs. He has the best creative mind among them. I told my sons that as long as they sent me a check every month and gave Miss Kay and me enough money to pay our bills, I really didn't need anything more. Now that the company has become famous worldwide, the checks are getting bigger and bigger every month. They're all getting rich out of the deal.

When the money started coming in, Miss Kay and I really didn't know what to do with it. We were like, "Whoa, the Almighty is blessing us in a new way." We decided to be generous and charitable and help as many people as we could. We're building schools in Africa and helping to finance mission trips to spread the Good News around the world. We were the same way when we didn't have any money. When I was making $225 a week, our house was always filled with people who were down on their luck. We shared the Good News with them, fed them, housed them, and gave them opportunities to turn their lives around. We never turned anyone away if they needed help and really wanted to help themselves. I like to think that since we did right when we didn't have much money, the blessings started pouring in once *Duck Dynasty* took off.

One day, I asked Miss Kay, "I know we're rich now, but when am I going to feel rich?" Her answer was: "Phil, we were content when were poor, so we won't ever feel rich." She was right.

Save your money, buy only what you need, give generously, and, most important, prepare yourself for God's inheritance.

4

---◆◇◆---

SOCIAL MEDIA

Fix No. 4: Mind Your Own Business

A recent study by International Data Corporation revealed that 50 percent of the American population uses some sort of smartphone. Now, I've never owned a cell phone and, rest assured, I never will. But from what I've seen over the last several years, smartphones only seem to make their users dumber. I laugh every time I see someone struggling to carry shopping bags and an umbrella through a parking lot on a rainy day while holding a cell phone to his ear. Hang up the phone, you idiot! You wouldn't believe how many times my sons Willie and Jep have dropped their iPhones in the water while we're duck hunting. Okay, tell me again exactly why you needed them in the duck blind. Were you going to call the ducks with your cell phones? It seems, from my vantage point, that most people spend a lot of time trying to find their cell phone!

Americans need to get off their cell phones—my sons included. Contrary to what you're thinking, you can live without them. I promise you can operate and function without them. I don't have one. You don't have to have one, either. And while you're at it, get off your desktop computer, laptop, iPad, tablet, reader, and whatever other mobile devices you own. I've never figured out how the computer, the very device that was supposed to revolutionize the way we live and save us so much time, ended up occupying so much of our time. Americans can't stay off them!

The IDC study revealed some alarming facts about Americans. Did you know that 79 percent of smartphone users reach for their devices within fifteen minutes of waking up? A majority of them—62 percent—don't even wait fifteen minutes! I have an idea: why don't you grab a Bible and read, or lie there in bed and pray or meditate for a few quiet moments? Hey, news flash, folks: I promise you it's the only quiet time you're probably going to get in this busy, busy world. Why don't you take advantage of a few moments of solitude and slow down, Jack?

I'm convinced that the Internet and social media in particular, the very things that were supposed to bring us closer together, have actually distanced us from each other more than ever before. They're destroying the social interaction among humans. We don't talk to anybody anymore, and we've isolated ourselves, spending most of our time in front of a computer or tapping the screens of our smartphones and tablets. We've become robots. In

1950, less than 10 percent of American households contained only one person. By 2012, almost 27 percent of households were a single person. Who needs a spouse or roommate when you have five hundred friends on Facebook or one thousand followers on Twitter? I don't get it.

And don't even get me started about online dating. Did you know there are actual online dating sites for ugly people, people who like to ride horses, people who like cats, people who dress up like clowns, adults who love to wear diapers, and people with food allergies? I'm not kidding! Hey, I realize there's probably someone out there for everybody—look at my brother Si for goodness' sake—but don't you think there's a better way to meet Mr. or Mrs. Right than by exchanging a few e-mails? Can't you meet a woman or man in church or school? How do you really know they're the one if you've never watched them pluck feathers from a duck or clean fish? Don't you at least need to know what they smell like? You really need to get to know a man or woman face-to-face, because it has been my observation that if people are mean, they get a lot meaner after they're married. Trust me, you're going to need more than a cell phone or computer to discover that part of someone's personality!

> I'm convinced that the Internet and social media in particular, the very things that were supposed to bring us closer together, have actually distanced us from each other more than ever before.

Sadly, we don't carry on conversations with our neighbors, our coworkers, or even our family members anymore. Instead of actually talking to them, we send each other text messages, tweets, direct messages, and e-mails. What happened to actually hearing a loved one's voice? The best days of my life were spent with my boys, brothers, and friends in a duck blind for hours, sharing stories and memories and laughing together as we waited for the ducks to come in. When was the last time you had a truly meaningful conversation with your spouse or children? When was the last time you walked next door to your neighbors' house, sat on the front porch, and talked with them over a glass of tea? We spend so much time on Twitter, My Page, Your Page, MyTube, YouTube, LinkedIn, LinkedOut, Pinterest, and all of these other social media sites that we don't have any worthwhile interaction with anyone. Instead of talking with our mouths, we're letting our fingers do the talking. It isn't healthy.

As someone who has never owned a cell phone or computer, I've wondered about the reasons behind the social media explosion in our country. The only answer I can come up with is that Americans are basically bored and nosy. Nowadays, minding your own business is extremely rare. I'm warning you, folks: if you don't put down your cell phones and get off Facebook and Twitter, digital dementia is right around the corner. Digital dementia is capturing our souls, and we're cultivating a generation of robotic nerds.

Social media and our desire to know everyone else's business are consuming us more and more every day. The IDC study revealed that 70 percent of smartphone users are frequent Facebook visitors, with more than half of them logging on every single day. On average, the study found, smartphone users visit the Facebook application 13.8 times per day, for two minutes and twenty-two seconds each time. And that's only while using their smartphones! As soon as they get home, I'm sure they're turning on their laptops and iPads. On average, Americans spend about twenty-three hours per week e-mailing, texting, and using social media. That's 14 percent of the time in a week!

Imagine what you could do with the time you're spending on your mobile devices and computers. You could actually talk to your spouse and kids, volunteer at a food bank or school, throw the football in the backyard, or take your kids hunting or fishing. Heck, some people spend so much time on Facebook that if they stopped they could actually get a job! But people rarely seem to put their cell phones down, no matter what they're doing. They check Facebook while they're shopping, while at the gym, and while cooking. People even use their cell phones while they're at the movies! Let me get this straight: you're going to get hosed for a ten-dollar ticket to the movies, and then you're going to spend the entire two hours looking at your phone? Hey, how about actually watching the movie?

I can't figure out why Americans are so preoccupied with what everyone else is up to. Evidently, people are starved for something they don't have or couldn't keep. They want to know what their friends are doing, where they're going, and what they're eating for dinner. It seems like we're envious of each other and dissatisfied with our own lives. Talk about putting yourself in a depression. Why would you want to know what your ex-girlfriend is doing in Texas or California? Or what kind of truck some guy you barely knew in high school bought? Do you know the worst part about social media? People don't know when to be quiet. Do I really need to know how many times you've flossed your teeth today or that you've lost forty-two pounds with some miracle diet drug? People on social media can't see you yawning from the boredom, so they keep yapping away.

According to researchers at the Pew Research Center, 73 percent of adults in the U.S. use some form of social media. Facebook alone has 1.19 billion users worldwide—more than three times the population of the United States! Think about that—one in every seven people in the world is using Facebook! I'm starting to think social media might be more addictive than cocaine and heroin.

> **Do I really need to know how many times you've flossed your teeth today or that you've lost forty-two pounds with some miracle diet drug?**

Americans can't seem to get enough of it, and social media is making us narcissistic and envious of others.

I'll never forget the time my son Jase told me he had millions of friends.

"Millions of friends, huh?" I asked him.

"Yeah, I'm up to two million friends on Facebook," he said.

"How is that?" I asked him. "How do you talk to every last one of them? How do you do that?"

Jase then asked me: "Dad, how many friends do you have?"

I held up one hand and simply told him, "Not as many as you."

When you log on to Facebook or some other social media site, how many of the people you're communicating with are really your friends? How many do you have meaningful relationships with? How many of those people can you actually share your problems and struggles with? Miss Kay is my best friend and we talk about everything. Hey, the woman loves me! I couldn't imagine jumping onto a computer and sharing my dirty laundry for the whole world to see. It doesn't make any sense to me.

Much of the reason some people are so attracted to social media is gossip. Gossip is kind of like a second bowl of duck gumbo. We know we don't need it and might even say we don't want it, but when it's within reach, most of us can't resist it. Gossip is the same way. We're humans and imperfect, and we can't seem to get enough of it. Most people want to know everything about everyone, regardless of how hurtful it might be. Proverbs 18:8 says, *"The words of a gossip are like choice morsels; they go down to the inmost parts."* Gossip is a sin, and it involves not only the person talking, but also the people listening and the ones who repeat what they heard. We have to remember that what comes from our mouths lets everyone know who we are and who we belong to. There are even gossip websites, and people hosting them have become millionaires, feasting on gossip and the intimate details of other people's lives.

Here's another thing: why do we now have to document every one of life's precious moments with a photograph on Facebook and Instagram? I can understand a grandmother wanting to see photographs of her grandchildren if she lives across the country or a wife wanting to see photos of her husband if he's stationed overseas in the military. Hey, even photos of birthday parties, weddings, and anniversaries are okay. But do we have to document every little moment of our lives? According to Facebook, more than 750 million photographs are uploaded to their site on a given weekend. Isn't that what our memories are for?

Gossip is kind of like a second bowl of duck gumbo. We know we don't need it and might even say we don't want it, but when it's within reach, most of us can't resist it.

We've become narcissistic, wanting to share everything with our "friends." We have to tell them what we're doing, what we're wearing, who we're with, and where we're going. Then we'll sit in front of the computer for hours to see how many friends "liked" or shared the photos.

I'm telling you: social media isn't for me. My code of life can be summed up in a few short statements. 1 Thessalonians 4:11–12 tells us: *"Make it your ambition to lead a quiet life: You should mind your own business and work with your hands, just as we told you, so that your daily life may win the respect of outsiders and so that you will not be dependent on anybody."* That's what Paul the Apostle told the Thessalonians as he was writing on behalf of the Father of the cosmos. Paul did not tell the Thessalonians to live noisy, chaotic lives. Instead, he told them to love each other and to make it their ambition to lead quiet lives. He told them to concentrate on their own lives, take care of their own jobs and responsibilities, and not meddle in the affairs of others. In other words, he told them not to be nosy.

I've made it my ambition to live a quiet life. Once the *Duck Dynasty* cameras are turned off for the final time, Miss Kay and I are still going to be living in the same place we were before, in the same house on the banks of the Ouachita River. I'm going to wake up every morning, spend most of my day in the woods or on the river, and then enjoy a quiet evening. There won't be a cell phone attached to my hip. I'm going to be doing the same things when I'm old and gray. Here is one of the few bits of advice I'm ever going to give the news media: Write anything you want about me, good or bad, on your websites and blogs. I don't own a cell phone or computer, so I'm not privy to that information. I'm not hearing you—ever! You might as well not say it.

I can promise you one thing: you'll never find me logging on to Facebook or Twitter or e-mailing or texting someone. If someone needs to talk to me, they know where I live. They can come talk to me face-to-face, instead of sending me a tweet of 140 characters or less. Seriously, what can you really say in less than 140 characters? We've become shallow and uninformed. If my friends and associates can't get to my house, then they can call me on the phone—the kind that's attached to the wall. Good luck getting me to answer it.

You have to understand that I've never e-mailed anybody in my life and have rarely written anyone a letter. One day, as I was walking through the warehouse of Duck Commander, I saw six women sitting in front of computers.

"What are y'all doing?" I asked them.

"We're answering your e-mails, Mr. Robertson," one of them told me.

"You're doing what?" I asked her.

"We're answering your mail, sir," she said.

"All of you?" I asked.

"Yes, all of us," she said.

Apparently, I was receiving thousands of e-mails every day. Miss Kay, Uncle Si, and each of my sons were getting nearly as many. I had no idea we had so many long-lost cousins in Nigeria or some other faraway land who were in desperate need of money. I had no idea I'd ever entered the Irish lottery. I could only shake my head and say, "Well, good grief."

One of the craziest things to me is the fact that *Duck Dynasty* has become a social media phenomenon. We love each and every one of our fans, and fortunately they love our show and family. But the show's popularity has turned our quiet lives into not-so-quiet lives. Hey, it's one of the hazards of reality TV. The irony of it to me is that millions of fans—and a lot of them are the people who are on Facebook, Twitter, and other social media—were probably attracted to the Robertson family because they saw us as people who minded our own business, worked hard, built duck calls, and loved God and each other. Maybe they thought we were interesting or maybe they thought we were weird. I like to think they were attracted to the fact that we live godly and productive lives. I've chosen to live my life kind of like Americans did fifty or sixty years ago. I think a lot of Americans would like to live the way their grandparents and great-grandparents did, when times were much more simple and a lot less stressful. But most Americans have been caught up in the rat race, and they're afraid to give up the conveniences of the twenty-first century. I think simpler lives are what a lot of people in America really want, but they've been consumed by the modern-day American culture. They're living wide open and romping and stomping to make money and climb their way to the top. It doesn't have to be that way.

We really need to decide what's important in our lives. Life doesn't have to be so complicated. We need to figure out the people we want to spend our time with and what we want to accomplish. We need to examine our commitments and declutter our lives. If we have stress coming out of our pores, we need to commit to doing less each day. Hey, it's okay to even do nothing every once in a while. Every one of us needs a vacation now and then. We need to slow down, eat slowly, and enjoy the moments we have with our families and friends—the ones who are physically with us! When you come home from work, turn off your cell phone, computer, and TV. Spend some quality time with your spouse and kids. Talk about your day and spend time with them outdoors. Learn to decompress and to not worry about the things that really don't matter. As it says in Proverbs 15:16, *"Better a little with the fear of the Lord than great wealth with turmoil."*

You can't imagine how many people across the country have told my family that their favorite part of *Duck Dynasty* is the end of the episodes, when the Robertson family is gathered around the long table in Miss Kay's dining room, sharing a meal together. After thanking the Lord for our food and blessings, we share stories and tales and laugh together as we enjoy our meal. It was always that way, even long before Hollywood decided it wanted to put a family of rednecks from Louisiana on national TV. If you look closely, you'll notice there's never a cell phone or iPad in sight. Not at my table, Jack!

Hey, it's okay to even do nothing every once in a while.

5

FAMILY

Fix No. 5: Raise Your Children in a Godly Environment

I have been on both sides of the fence when it comes to parenting. During my first twenty-eight years on earth, I was not a God-fearing man and lived a lifestyle of romping, stomping, and ripping. I was not a very good father and was more concerned about my own sinful desires than I was about my family. My son Alan was ten years old before I repented, so some damage was probably done. He was not reared in a godly family environment during the first part of his life, and I think that experience probably led to some problems later in his life.

But after I repented and accepted Jesus Christ as my Lord and Savior, our boys lived in a family structure and a godly environment. From the time I repented, I tried to put the Bible into practice in our everyday lives. Even though my sons Jase and

Willie were still relatively young—Jep hadn't even come along yet—I tried to teach them the difference between right and wrong, based on what I'd read in the Scripture. Second Timothy 3:16 says: *"All Scripture is God-breathed and is useful for teaching, rebuking, correcting and training in righteousness."* The Bible was the blueprint for their upbringing.

More than anything, I wanted my boys to know that I loved their mother, loved them, and loved God, which I had not done during the first twenty-eight years of my life. Love for God, our spouses, and our children is a prerequisite to teaching our kids to choose the right path in life, training them to follow the path, and correcting them when they stray

> More than anything, I wanted my boys to know that I loved their mother, loved them, and loved God.

off the path. Nothing is more important than love. They must know we love God, our spouses, and them. They have to see it through our actions and not only hear us say it. It's hard for them to see that we love them when we're mean to their mother or father.

As a father, I didn't believe I should exasperate my boys while trying to instill obedience in them. I got this message straight from the pages of the Bible. Ephesians 6:4 says, *"Fathers, do not exasperate your children; instead, bring them up in the training and instruction of the Lord."* You can't put rule upon rule in front of them and expect them to follow every one of them. They're children and they're going to step out of line every once in a while.

That's what kids do. When my boys were growing up, there were only three rules in our house: no disrespecting their mother, no physical fighting, and no tearing up good equipment. Any violation of the rules resulted in a punishment of three licks, no questions asked. I didn't even have to tell my boys not to disrespect me; they knew it was unthinkable and realized the consequences of doing it. But they knew what the rules were, and they were easy to follow. They knew what I expected from them in terms of their behavior.

Any rebuking we do as a parent should come from our desire for their best and for their safety. When Jase was in diapers and crawling around the floor, I constantly had to tell him not to stick his fingers into electrical outlets. Every time he reached for a 110-volt electrical socket, I swatted his hand away and told him, "No!" Obviously, I didn't want him to be electrocuted to death, and I wanted to teach him that there was imminent danger. There was always a lesson when I scolded them. We lived on a river and my boys knew that no one could go to the boat ramp until he learned to swim like a fish. My boys learned when they were very young that when the man said no, he was only looking out for them. When they were older, they didn't question me when I told them they couldn't ride motorcycles or do other dangerous things. They knew I had their best interests at heart.

Really, that was the system of discipline in the Robertson household. And you need to know this: *discipline* does not mean "punishment"; it means "teaching and training."

My love for my boys' mother, my love for them, and my love for God outweighed the punishment and taught them what they needed to know. God ran the entire household and then me. If you run your house from the top down, it goes pretty smoothly. I think it was easier for Miss Kay because she only had to say, "I'm telling your dad," whenever a skirmish broke out or one of the boys talked back to her. Disciplining, correcting, and teaching your children requires consistency and good communication between the parents. It's a cooperative effort, and it's one of your most important roles on earth. Miss Kay never questioned me when I disciplined our sons. We had a united, strong front, and they knew Mom and Dad were undivided.

I think the fact that our boys weren't covered up with rules allowed them to become independent and learn right from wrong on their own. I wasn't very rough on my boys. I've seen some dads—even good Christian men—who are too tough on their children. They put too many rules in place, so the kids rebel because they feel their independence is being taken away. It takes good communication, and you can't ask your kids to do anything you wouldn't do. We didn't have a curfew in our house, but my boys knew they were expected to be up, dressed, and ready for school by seven o'clock every morning. They had alarm clocks and got up on their own. They knew they were supposed to respect their teachers like they respected their parents, and many of their teachers and principals called Miss Kay and me to tell us that our boys were some of the most well-behaved children they'd ever had in their schools.

We had a simple, biblical system of discipline in our home. We didn't overdo it and didn't have a long list of rules on the icebox. Miss Kay and I worked hard to ensure one thing—that our boys obeyed us. We started when they were young, and it didn't take them long to adapt to our rules. I think the really critical time for child rearing is from the time kids are toddlers until about the ninth grade. If obedience and respect for you and other elders isn't built into children by the time they reach the ninth grade, I'm afraid it's probably too late. Unfortunately, rebellion and disobedience are probably going to run their course. If your children don't respect you because of parental neglect, you're going to suffer a lot of heartache.

I think the last time I licked one of my boys was when Alan was fifteen. He and three of his buddies went camping on our property one night, drank some beer, and then decided to tear up some of our neighbors' mailboxes. When I learned about it the next morning, I went and got all of them and lined them up in front of my truck. I gave each of the four boys three licks each, even though I didn't even know one of them. All four of the boys are now godly men; it didn't ruin their self-esteem. I think you have to discipline your children if you want them to be obedient to God and you.

Now, don't get me wrong. My boys weren't perfect. There will be glitches; it's part of life. Alan left home for two years and moved to New Orleans because we didn't approve of his lifestyle. He eventually came back and asked for forgiveness. When Alan came home, he told me, "Dad, I blew it." I hugged him and told him that I loved him. "Come on, let's eat us a big steak," I told him. "I'm glad you're back."

My youngest son, Jep, also had some problems after high school. He was using alcohol and prescription pills and we had a family intervention to confront his problems. When we were finished, Jep asked us why it took us so long to intervene and thanked us for saving his life. We had our problems, but each of my boys returned to the right path. The bottom line is they knew we were there and loved them. It's not like we'll never have any issues with our children, but we deal with them in a godly manner. Eventually, all of the early discipline pays off. Now that my boys are parents and grandparents, they're pulling from what they learned from us.

Did our system of discipline work well? It's one of the most beautiful things I've ever seen. Children have to see a structure in place. In our house, there was a patriarch and a matriarch, a mom and a dad. God has to be at the top. You have to do what the Almighty said to do: *"Start children off on the way they should go, and even when they are old they will not turn from it"* (Proverbs 22:6). Before Miss Kay and I realized it, we looked up and our boys had graduated from high school and college and were off starting their own families. Now they have their own children and grandchildren. Here's the real beauty of the system:

my grandkids and great-grandkids are as well behaved as my boys were. Sometimes, when we're eating in a restaurant, other patrons will come over and compliment us on their behavior.

I've been amazed at how disciplined my grandkids and great-grandkids are. You read and hear about the horror stories of children who are involved with TV shows and movies. Some of the most famous child actors are destroyed by fortune and fame. Our grandchildren and great-grandchildren have been blessed

> It's not like we'll never have any issues with our children, but we deal with them in a godly manner.

with a lot more than my boys ever had. We jumped into the teeth of the tiger with *Duck Dynasty*, but I couldn't have asked for anything better. It's a grind, and our grandchildren have accepted the responsibility with the utmost professionalism. They haven't let the blessings and celebrity go to their heads. I know everyone thinks they have the best kids and grandkids, but I've been amazed by this bunch. Willie's son John Luke is leading a teenage church group and has brought many kids to Jesus. Willie's daughter, Sadie, is writing a book and has her own fashion line that produces appropriate clothing for teenage girls. Jase's sons, Reed and Cole, are very involved in our church and are leaders at their school. I'm so proud of each of my grandchildren. I'm also very proud of my boys for the way they've raised their kids.

You really don't realize how strong your family structure is until big money starts flowing in every direction and everybody starts using their talents. None of us are envious of one another, and we realize how important each and every one of us is to the success of *Duck Dynasty*. You have to be a pretty tight bunch to step into something like this. I know this: a person had better know who they are and Whom they belong to before stepping into entertainment. If you don't, you might come out on the other side and not even be recognizable. People tend to go nuts when they get involved with Hollywood. Your roots had better be pretty deep to keep things in the right perspective. You better know your identity, or Hollywood will corrupt you.

I really hope America can return to raising children in godly homes and environments. At some point during the last thirty or forty years, Americans stopped teaching, correcting, and disciplining (or training) their children, and now we're seeing the results. They aren't good. Many of our children are out of control and have no respect for authority. It's almost like pulling teeth to get some American parents to correct their children. Hey, it has almost gotten to the point in this country where you can't correct them. Some people claim it's child abuse to spank their little behinds and make them behave. I've come to realize that human beings despise correction and discipline. We love to just let her rip with no restraint.

We have to remember that Jesus Christ died for us because of our sins. But when God tells us we have to live a life of restraint and self-control, we don't want to do it. As a result, we're not teaching, correcting, and disciplining our children to live lives of obedience. For the last fifty years or so, we've been churning out a generation of nerds. The men in our country face some special challenges. With no discipline or restraint, look at the crop of men we've produced. Whatever happened to manhood? Some fathers teach their sons to shave. Others teach them how to be men. Teach your boys how to be men.

I think the most important values we can teach our children are a healthy fear of God and the importance of hard work. Too many of our children are no longer willing to work for what they want. They feel they're entitled to every new gadget and toy because we've spoiled them and didn't teach them that you have to work for what you want. I think that's why America turned into a nation of entitlement. It's the scourge of work. Our children want to live their lives but don't want any pain from hard work—only the pleasure. Too many of our children never experience blood, sweat, and tears. We want everyone to feel like they've won no matter what. Our society tells us we can't have winners and losers because it hurts our children's self-esteem. We can no longer discipline our children or put them to work because it might hurt their feelings. Well, we've created a generation of fat, lazy children as a result. When they grow to become adults, they're still looking for their mamas and daddies—or the government—to bail them out. We need to get back to teaching our children personal responsibility and the virtues of hard work.

If we're going to save our children, we have to put God back into the equation. When I went to grade school, we prayed before the start of every school day. Now you can't even pray in schools or at school-sponsored events like football games. Since our schools no longer teach our children family values and godliness, it's up to us to ensure it happens—

> We have no impact on people outside of Jesus when we're inside the church building.

it's really been our responsibility all along. Our children's brains are like computers. They're going to be programmed by what we put into them. If we leave Jesus Christ and godly values out of what we're teaching them, they'll grow up to be adults whose brains are filled with filth.

It's up to us as believers to help get American families back into churches and Sunday school classes. Those of us who do attend church don't do enough outside of the church buildings. The American model of Christianity is to attend church on Sunday morning, Sunday night, and Wednesday night—and only a small segment of the population goes to church that frequently. But we have to remember that we have no impact on people outside of Jesus when we're inside the church building. Instead of the church being salt and light in our culture, too many of our church pews are sitting empty on Sundays. We Christians have to be that salt and light during our everyday lives.

We never forced Christianity on our boys. We prayed that they would make the decision to accept Jesus Christ as their Lord and Savior, but we never told them it was expected of them. Miss Kay and I taught them, instructed them, counseled them, and answered any questions they had about our faith.

Most important, we lived our lives so our boys would see how Christians live. When the time came when one of my boys asked me about Jesus, I shared the Good News with him, and eventually I baptized every one of them. If your children are having doubts about their faith, liken it to when they were only young children. Ask them to remember the first time they jumped into the swimming pool. As we stood in the pool, encouraging them to jump into our arms, they had to have faith that we wouldn't let them fall to the bottom. Then ask them to imagine the power that Jesus Christ has to prevent them from falling in life.

Look, you're basically going to be able to influence your children for about twenty years, maybe a little bit longer. Start at an early age and teach them about God and Jesus, love and forgiveness, peace and patience, goodness and gentleness. Be imitators of God, forgive each other, and live a life filled with love. Love your children, discipline them, and teach, correct, rebuke, and train them. Do it very carefully. Remember, the greatest gift you can give your children is love. More than anything else, always make sure they know that you love them.

PART TWO

HOT TOPICS

6

POLITICS

Fix No. 6: Elect Godly Men

Shortly after my last book, *Happy, Happy, Happy*, was published in May 2013, I was asked to sign a couple of copies for former U.S. presidential candidates John McCain and Ross Perot. I was told that McCain and Perot like the way I operate, and I have immense respect for both men. McCain was a war hero in Vietnam and is a longtime U.S. senator from Arizona. Perot, who ran for U.S. president twice in the 1990s, became a self-made billionaire by building a fortune in computers. I was surprised that they wanted to read my book. So here's the inscription that I wrote to each of them: "Based on my observations, my conclusion of our current political situation is one word: embarrassing."

Now, I love my country and every one of my fellow citizens, but there are some things about America that are flat-out embarrasing. And it starts with the people who are running our country in Washington, DC, and the people who are putting them there.

I don't consider myself a Republican or a Democrat, a left-winger or a right-winger, conservative or liberal. I consider myself a Christocrat because I advocate the principles of God's Word and God's government. My obedience to God is much more important than my loyalty to any political party, platform, or ideology. I know that only Jesus can resurrect me from the dead, so only He should govern me. Now, I'll follow the laws and rules of this country and be a good, taxpaying U.S. citizen, but I ultimately answer to only one higher power and that's the Almighty. No government can thwart His will.

Regardless of what you might have heard or read over the last six years, change comes only by repenting and hope comes only by faith in the resurrection of Jesus Christ. If you truly want change and hope in America, we have to put godly men back in Washington, DC. I don't believe you should vote for a politician unless they will at least mention God. I also believe that at some point during a political campaign, the candidate needs to say, "I'm running because I love you and I'm really concerned about our nation." I think it's time for the people that we elect to represent us to tell us they love us. It would make me feel a lot better about the process and

> **My obedience to God is much more important than my loyalty to any political party, platform, or ideology.**

what's going on with our government. If I knew the politicians actually loved me, I might have a better feeling about where our country is headed. I certainly don't like the direction it's headed now, that's for sure.

When I consider America's national deficit, our system of entitlements, and all of the problems we're having around the world, I'm absolutely sick about what's going on in Washington, DC. But Americans have to realize that whatever happens on Capitol Hill and in the White House is actually a reflection of the ones who put them there. And in America today, there are more ungodly people than there are godly folks. Ungodliness is ruling our country. It's the electorate that we're seeing in our nation's capital. The problem is not just our elected officials—it's the ones who put them there. Our nation elected them and they are an exact representation of who we are as a country. The people of America put them in office, so we need to quit bellyaching, griping, and complaining about them. The reason they're in our government to begin with is because ungodly people elect ungodly politicians. Elected officials in a democracy are simply replicas of the electorate. They are a reflection of who our country is made of. We are the problem.

> I believe that at some point during a political campaign, the candidate needs to say, "I'm running because I love you and I'm really concerned about our nation."

When people don't say yes to Jesus, they are unable to say no when they need to. When people lose the ability to say no to sin, they end up with the depraved leading the depraved down the road to tyranny and finally to utter destruction.

We're the problem, we really are. It's America at large that's at fault. When we evaluate the officials in Washington, DC, we are really only considering the evidence of the problem. When our nation puts them in office, we all feel the wrath of our own sin being put upon us. We say, "Boy, we're feeling a lot of wrath from this and a lot of money is coming out of our pockets. What in the world?" You have to remember that they are but a picture of the people who put them there. The ungodly put the ungodly in office. And now we're expecting them to be godly and treat us with love and kindness? It is impossible for the ungodly to elect the ungodly and then expect godliness to come from them. The corrupt elect the corrupt and the corruption continues. The depraved elect the depraved and the depravity continues. If you want kindness, love, peace, patience, goodness, and faithfulness—the characteristics you will find in godly men and women—you better get godly in a hurry and elect as many godly politicians as you can. When the biggest requirement for running for public office in this country is simply stockpiling a huge war chest of money to ensure a candidate can win, it shows that the foundation of our political system is broken. What about a candidate's character, morals, and integrity? Does what's inside the candidate's head not matter?

There's no use in arguing about the current state of our government. Political debates in this country have become nothing but televised shouting matches. The political talking heads on TV do nothing more than try to shout over each other. We need to rise above the vitriol and learn to love the people who disagree with us. We need to love our neighbor who believes in abortion, we need to love the atheist who wants to keep creationism out of schools, and we need to love the recent college graduate who wants to take down the nativity scene at the courthouse. It does us no good to argue with them. As it says in Second Timothy 2:23–26, *"Don't have anything to do with foolish and stupid arguments, because you know they produce quarrels. And the Lord's servant must not be quarrelsome but must be kind to everyone, able to teach, not resentful. Opponents must be gently instructed, in the hope that God will grant them repentance leading them to a knowledge of the truth, and that they will come to their senses and escape from the trap of the devil, who has taken them captive to do his will."* All we can do is love the nonbelievers and try to turn them.

> **If you want kindness, love, peace, patience, goodness, and faithfulness in your elected officials, you better get godly in a hurry and elect as many godly politicians as you can.**

You might ask, "Well, how do we change it and get that bunch out of Washington, DC?" You yourself are going to have to repent, turn to Jesus, and put people in Washington, DC, who fear God and love their neighbors. If we don't change, we're going to have more of the same forevermore until it finally collapses. Don't think it can happen? Look at the Roman Empire.

The Romans were the greatest military force in the history of the world. They conquered lands from England to Africa and from Syria to Spain during the first and second centuries. But then Rome rotted from within because of sin, political strife, disease, greed, and corruption. The Romans toppled themselves, and now Rome is only shoving out pizzas.

> We need to rise above the vitriol and learn to love the people who disagree with us.

I truly believe that America will become ruins if it doesn't change. We have met the enemy and it's us. Where there is no Jesus, you end up in a society where everything is political. That's why there's so much political correctness in our country today. Our politicians and electorate think all of our problems can be fixed with politics. But politics isn't the answer; Jesus, repentance, and the elimination of sins are the only answers. Sadly, arrogance, corruption, greed, depravity, and degradation are now the centerpieces of the American dream. America is reeling, teetering, rotting, and struggling within herself. She, America, is fighting for her existence. She is in the beginning of her collapse under the weight of her sin. All of the great republics before us succumbed to the same forces of evil she is now experiencing. Looking at America is like watching a rotting carcass: it smells, and the vultures will gather around her until she finally disappears.

Now, I'm only an average-intelligence man, and I'm sure the intellectuals and academics are going to disagree with me, but I'm of the belief that two principles are the driving forces behind most of the political structures on earth, especially the current one in the United States. The government puts forth these two principles, marries them, and then believes they can fix anything. It basically comes down to this: give us *money* and *intellect*, and we can accomplish anything. That's pretty much the standard modus operandi of America. The U.S. government tells us they have the best people, the gurus with all of the brains. They tell us to listen to them because they know what's best for the populace. What do they keep saying? "Trust us! Trust our intellect." Well, if that in fact is true and all they need is intellect and money, then how in the world are we $17 trillion in the hole and counting? You don't get that far in the hole by being smart. Find out what the term *balanced budget* means, Jack!

Politicians who claim we can spend our way out of debt are at fault. They are sickened fools. What's the difference between intellect and wisdom? Intellect leads to the slaughter of human beings while they are in their mothers' wombs. Intellect, as it turns out, has plunged America into $17 trillion worth of debt. Wisdom causes one to fear God! Whoa, even a man of average intelligence can be wise.

Why does Congress continue to raise taxes? I thought their premise was that if politicians were smart enough and threw enough money at something, they could solve anything. But they haven't fixed much of anything lately, and they keep dipping into our pockets for more money. Our government officials always say the same thing: give us more money and we can fix it. Our government believes it can fix every one of our enemies worldwide by giving them more humanitarian aid. The U.S. believes it can buy its friends through nation building, foreign intervention, and preemptive war. Well, how has it worked out in Afghanistan and Iraq? We have rapidly growing domestic entitlement programs that aren't sustainable and rarely accomplish their stated goals. Politicians believe they can fix our educational system with more funding. Yet, according to recent worldwide testing results, American high school students rank behind students from countries like Slovakia, Portugal, Vietnam, and Russia in math. Our students rank near the bottom in science, too. Are you kidding me? It's embarrassing. These statistics fly in the face of what the politicians are telling us—that money can solve our problems.

I understand that a political structure is, in fact, going to be what ends up steering a country in the way it should go—or at least the way the politicians want to make it go. While some issues can be politically fixed, I believe spiritual, godly men would be much more effective politicians and lawmakers than ungodly men. The reason the current political parties rarely, if ever, change their minds is because there is no gospel in any of their arguments—none! Hey, Washington, DC, quit shoveling us horse manure, repent, and turn to God, and our nation might survive.

Our founding fathers were godly men and created the

greatest republic in the history of mankind. It only took us two hundred and thirty-eight years to screw it up! Great men like Benjamin Franklin, Thomas Jefferson, James Madison, and Daniel Webster knew that morals and religion were necessary to form the government they were establishing. George Washington, the very first president of the United States, said in a Thanksgiving proclamation in New York on October 3, 1789: "It is the duty of all Nations to acknowledge the Providence of Almighty God, to obey his will, to be grateful for his benefits, and humbly to implore his protection and favor: and whereas both Houses of Congress have, by their joint Committee, requested me 'to recommend to the People of the United States, a day of public Thanksgiving and Prayer, to be observed by acknowledging with grateful hearts the many signal favors of Almighty God, especially by affording them an opportunity peaceably to establish a form of government for their safety and happiness.'"

Washington, who was one of our greatest presidents and generals, repeatedly talked about God's blessings on America throughout his life. In his farewell address on September 19, 1796, he said: "Of all the dispositions and habits which lead to political prosperity, religion and morality are indispensable supports. In vain would that man claim the tribute of patriotism who should labor to subvert these great pillars of human happiness." Washington believed religion and morality were the pillars on which America would stand and flourish. Well, they were for

"Of all the dispositions
and habits which lead to political
prosperity, religion and morality
are indispensable supports."
—President George Washington

the first two hundred years of our country's existence, but it's not that way anymore.

Washington wasn't the only founding father who believed religion and morality would be the backbone of America. John Adams, the second U.S. president, wrote to the officers of the First Brigade of the Third Division of the Militia of Massachusetts on October 11, 1798: "Our Constitution was made only for a moral and religious people. It is wholly inadequate to the government of any others." In an August 28, 1811, letter to Dr. Benjamin Rush, Adams also wrote: "Religion and virtue are the only foundations, not only of republicanism and all free government, but of social felicity under all governments and in all the combinations of human society."

And there were others. In a speech at Plymouth, Massachusetts, on December 22, 1820, Daniel Webster, a U.S. senator and secretary of state, said: "Whatever makes men good Christians, makes them good citizens." John Jay, the first chief justice of the United States, wrote in an October 12, 1816, letter to Pennsylvania lawmaker John Murray: "Real Christians will abstain from violating the rights of others, and therefore will not provoke war. Almost all nations have peace or war at the will and pleasure of rulers whom they do not elect, and who are not always wise and virtuous. Providence has given to our people the choice of their rulers, and it is the duty, as well as the privilege and interest, of our Christian nation to select and prefer Christians for their rulers."

Abraham Lincoln, our sixteenth president and the man who fought to end slavery in America, said in his farewell speech on February 11, 1861: "Without the assistance of that Divine Being, who ever attended [George Washington], I cannot succeed. With that assistance I cannot fail. Trusting in Him, who can go with me, and remain with you and be every where for good, let us confidently hope that all will yet be well. To His care commending you, as I hope in your prayers you will commend me, I bid you an affectionate farewell."

After reading the ideologies and beliefs of our founding fathers and other U.S. presidents, I'm convinced the solution to America's problem is not a political fix. It's a spiritual fix. Therefore, we have to start from the bottom, and the American people have to be won over. We have to elect leaders who are spiritual to become our politicians, and then they'll fix the country. I'm not suggesting something new. I'm only reminding people of what was said more than two hundred years ago, when our once-great country was founded.

Of course, you can go back to the Bible and find the same thing. As it says in Exodus 18:21, *"Select capable men from all the people—men who fear God, trustworthy men who hate dishonest gain—and appoint them as officials over thousands, hundreds, fifties and tens."* We have a few good men and women like that in Washington, DC, today, but not nearly enough of them. You get evil leaders in power and the next thing you know the whole thing falls apart. When the populace becomes evil, we elect evil leaders, and there you go. America is still a superpower in the world, but it has third-world leaders. Our leadership has to change.

I am convinced the battle for America will be won from the bottom up, from the people to the politicians, and not from the top down. When the converted outnumber the corrupt, America will win. Unless the people change, the politicians who are the hogs at the trough will keep going to Washington, DC. When the converted win, our families will be back together under one roof, parents will start raising their children again, and everyone will feel a responsibility to work and contribute to society. It has often been said that America's political structure is a "government of laws, not men." But bad men are more than capable of corrupting good laws, and good men will rule well in the absence of good laws. We don't have enough good men in Washington, DC, anymore.

> I am convinced the battle for America will be won from the bottom up, from the people to the politicians, and not from the top down.

Right now, there are enough ungodly people in America to control the country. There are more of them and not enough of us to turn the country around. In fact, there are more of them than us for the first time in America's history, in my opinion. When Jesus returns, righteousness will rule once again, this time forever. So here's my advice, America: go forth, do the best you can, and try to turn the population toward God—hoping that when we get enough godly people, we'll put godly men in government. What if that fails and we're not able to accomplish it? Well, just remember that you who belong to Jesus are the kingdom of God and the kingdom of God will last forever, even if our beloved America should fall.

7

RACE

Fix No. 7: Judge a Man by His Heart, Not the Color of His Skin

If you really want to know what kind of a person a particular man or woman is, the best way to do it might be to ask everyone who has ever come into contact with them. What does his wife say about him when he is not around? What does her husband say about her? What do their children say about them? Ask all of their friends and everyone they do business with what kind of person they are. Ask anyone: "Hey, what about this person?" Interview every last individual who has known them over their lifetime, and you would probably be able to come to some conclusion about who they really are. You know what? That is what people should do if they want to find out who the real Phil Robertson is.

After *GQ* magazine published a story about *Duck Dynasty* in December 2013, some people criticized me for quoting Bible verses relating to sin after a reporter asked me a question about homosexuality (you'll read more about that later). Other people were upset about comments I made about growing up with African Americans in Louisiana during the civil rights era. Look, folks, we can argue until the end of the earth about what constitutes sin in the eyes of God. Our opinions about certain lifestyles might be different, but I can promise you one thing: there isn't a racist bone in my body. There never has been and never will be. I'm confident anyone who has known me during the last four decades, including many African Americans who were and are among my closest friends, would tell you the same thing.

Before I converted and accepted Jesus Christ as my Lord and Savior, I was sexually immoral and committed a lot of other sins. I was an idolater, adulterer, thief, drunkard, and slanderer. I was guilty of fits of rage, jealousy, impurity, and dishonesty. And to top it all off, I was given to hatred no matter the color, whether someone was white, black, Indian, or Asian. There was no racism in my life even then. I hated everyone equally if they tried to slow down my sinful life. That is the kind of man I was during the first twenty-eight years of my life. But the new me, which came to be because of the grace of God during the last forty years, learned to *love*. I can't go back and undo the mistakes I made in the past, but God undid them for me. He can undo yours for you, too. If people are given to racism, whatever color they are, remind them of Acts 17:24–26: *"The God who made the world and everything in it is the Lord of heaven and earth and does not live in temples built by human hands. And he is not served by human hands, as if he needed anything. Rather, he himself gives everyone life and breath and everything else. From one man he made all the nations, that they should inhabit the whole earth."*

According to the Scripture, God made every nation from one man—Adam. The text says that every one of us—whether our skin is black, white, red, yellow, blue, or green—came from the same dude. That contradicts what my Sociology 101 professor tried to teach me at Louisiana Tech University. He tried to tell me that there are three groups of humans in the world: Caucasian, Negroid, and Mongoloid. But the Bible says God made every one of us from one person, and I don't know what color skin Adam had and neither do you. However, I doubt very seriously that he was Caucasian because he lived in what is now Iraq, so I'm guessing he looked like someone of Middle Eastern descent.

> The Bible says that every one of us—whether our skin is black, white, red, yellow, blue, or green—came from the same dude.

Some of us need to get off the color code in America and take to heart, once and for all: *"For God so loved the world that he gave his one and only Son, that whoever believes in him shall not perish but have eternal life"* (John 3:16). We need to understand that we're all humans and Americans, regardless of how we might look.

During the interview with the *GQ* reporter, I told him that I believed our country's founding fathers were Bible-loving and godly men. He reminded me that many of the founding fathers approved of slavery.

"Do you believe in slavery?" he asked me.

I told him I absolutely did not.

Then the reporter asked me if I ever witnessed an African American being mistreated by a white person while growing up in the South. Now, you have to remember that I spent much of my youth in Dixie, Louisiana, during the civil rights struggle. I told the reporter that I'd never personally witnessed an African American being mistreated by a white person or a white person being mistreated by an African American for that matter. I never saw it happen. I grew up in a very small farming community in Caddo Parish, which is in the northwest corner of Louisiana, near the Arkansas border. I never witnessed any friction between races, and I grew up with whites and blacks. That was my personal experience at that time in my life.

But that doesn't mean I'm naïve enough to think that African Americans weren't badly mistreated for more than a century—even after the Thirteenth Amendment abolished slavery in the United States in 1865. The days of slavery and then Jim Crow laws in the South were the darkest days in our country's history. Where I grew up, segregation laws were in place, and whites and blacks attended separate schools and used separate restrooms. I'll never forget the first time I saw a "colored" restroom. I looked at it and thought to myself, *Separate bathrooms? What kind of idiot came up with that?* I know African Americans were badly

mistreated in the South, including in Louisiana. Historians have
documented thousands of cases
of horrific lynchings, beatings,
and murders in the South during
the twentieth century, but I never
saw an incident with my own eyes,

African Americans were badly mistreated in the South, including thousands of cases of horrific lynchings, beatings, and murders, but I never saw an incident with my own eyes.

which is what I told the *GQ* reporter. If it ever happened in my
neck of the woods, it didn't occur in the open because I never
saw it or heard about it. At the time, I didn't know what Jim
Crow laws were because I was only a kid. I was born into the
culture and didn't know any better.

My parents weren't racists by any stretch of the imagination,
and they taught my brothers and sisters and me to love everyone
unconditionally—skin color was not a factor. For much of my
childhood, we lived next door to Melinda and Charlie Randall,
who were African Americans, and we loved them and they loved
us. We played with their children almost every day, and they
were among our closest friends. We broke bread together and
hunted and fished together. My brother Silas taught many of
the Randall children how to swim in a watering hole near our
farm. My family and their family were among the poorest in
town; maybe that's what brought us together. Though nobody
ever told us we were poor.

The African American families who lived in Dixie when
I lived there were some of the most generous people I've ever

known. When my father broke his back while working on an oil rig and was immobilized for more than a year, a few of the African American families in town took up a collection during the holidays because they knew my parents wouldn't have the money to buy us kids presents. When we woke up Christmas morning, there was a basket stuffed full of fruit, canned goods, and candies on the front porch. At the time, we didn't know where it came from, but we ate every bit of it, that's for sure. The black families had decided to help a neighbor in need because they loved us, and I know my parents would have done the same for them.

Even though my parents didn't have much in terms of money and material possessions, they were always generous and hospitable, because that's what the Bible tells us to do. Our house sat across the road from railroad tracks, and I suspect that every "hobo"—as we called them then—who traveled that particular line of tracks must have known where the Robertson house was located. My mother never turned away anyone who was in need of food, water, or clean clothes. When trains stopped in Dixie, many of the men jumped out of the rail cars and made their way to our back door. They ate whatever we were eating, whether they were black or white, and us kids would gather in the kitchen to watch them. My mother was a brave woman for inviting so many strangers into our home.

One morning, I asked one of the men, "How is that plate of squirrels and dumplings?"

"I've tasted better," he told me.

My mama was so mad. When he left, she said he was the most ungrateful hobo she'd ever met. I'm pretty sure she still fed him the next time he came to our back door.

From the time I was in the seventh grade until the ninth grade during the late 1950s, I worked in the cotton fields every summer for a farmer in Dixie. We started our workdays about six o'clock in the morning and didn't finish until around six o'clock in the evening. My brothers Tommy, Jimmy Frank, and Harold worked in the cotton fields with me, along with the farmer's son, who was a good friend. We picked cotton and hoed weeds all day long, often carrying one-hundred-pound bags of cotton more than a quarter mile as we navigated our way through the rows of cotton. It was a long, miserable day in the cotton fields, especially when the hot Louisiana sun was beating on our backs in July and August. About the only thing that distracted us from our miserable work was hearing the beautiful sounds of the African American workers singing hymns as they picked cotton. It's the prettiest sound you'll ever hear. We stood shoulder to shoulder with them, lining each row of cotton, and we drank from the same water buckets and worked under the same rules. We made three dollars a day and they were paid three dollars a day. All of the money my brothers and I earned went back to our parents.

The African Americans who worked in the cotton fields with us were some of the strongest and best people I ever ran with on the face of the earth. Their families were intact and they loved God. They loved us and we loved them. I worked with them for about three summers and they were the salt of the earth. The thing I'll always remember is that many of the African Americans I knew attended church every Sunday and stayed there for nearly the entire day. There was a small church with a tall steeple on the edge of the cotton field, and they piled in there every Sunday morning. I mean they were there from sunrise to sunset! They often ate lunch and dinner on the church lawn. The reason they worshipped for so long, in my opinion, is that during a time when their civil rights were being trampled, they embraced the one thing that couldn't be taken away from them—their faith.

Basically, the people who were around us, whether they were black or white, were good people. None of us were rich, but we were content and worked extremely hard for what we had. There was very little mischief, certainly not the kind of stuff we're dealing with nowadays. Life was slow and easy. It was only ten years or so after World War II, and I think people had a gut full of killing and hate. Like I said earlier, I know there was racism throughout the South when I was a kid, but I never saw it in the little circle where I lived. Maybe I was insulated because I was around so many good people. We simply loved God and one another, worked hard to make a living, and all seemed to get along. I like to think it was because we all had the same kind of morals and values, even though we might have looked different.

> During a time when their civil rights were being trampled, they embraced the one thing that couldn't be taken away from them—their faith.

Miss Kay and I tried to raise our boys the same way our parents raised us. We welcomed all kinds of people from different backgrounds into our home, fed them, and shared the Good News with them, regardless of their financial status, their faith, or the color of their skin. Some of my boys' best friends growing up were African Americans. Willie's best friend in high school, Paul Lewis, was an unbelievable basketball player. He and Willie were nearly inseparable, and before too long Willie and Jase were spending most of their time playing basketball with Paul in a predominantly African American neighborhood in West Monroe, Louisiana. One night, a policeman stopped near the basketball court where they were playing and waved for Willie to come over.

"Boy, what are you doing over here so late?" he asked Willie. "Don't you know it's dangerous?"

"Man, I know everybody in this neighborhood," Willie told him. "I'll be fine."

Willie often spent the night at Paul's house, and Paul spent many nights at our house. After graduating from high school, Paul was given a full scholarship to play college basketball at Southeastern Louisiana University in Hammond. We all watched Paul play against Shaquille O'Neal and LSU one time, and we were so excited to see him playing on TV. Sadly, Paul was arrested for selling dope and transporting drugs in Texas in 1995. He strayed from how his parents had raised him to be and got involved with the wrong crowd. It was a big mistake, and he ended up paying a steep price. When Paul was being sentenced in a federal court in Texas, I stood in front of the judge and begged for leniency. I think the judge was surprised to see me in his courtroom.

"Mr. Robertson, are you condoning drug trafficking?" he asked me.

"No, we need to get drugs off our streets," I told him. "But I'm pleading for mercy in this case. I know this boy and his family. They're good people. I love him, and we'll help him turn his life around."

Despite my pleas, the judge sentenced Paul to fourteen years in prison, which he spent in federal facilities in Arkansas, Louisiana, and Texas. When Paul was finally released from prison, Willie had him moved to a halfway house in West Monroe. Willie hired Paul at Duck Commander, and he's now our warehouse manager. We helped him get a truck and moved him into a trailer home on my property. I knew he was a good kid who made a terrible mistake, and I was going to do everything in my power to help him turn his life around. Paul and another one of our Duck Commander employees, Krystle, fell in love and were married by Alan in my yard. Willie was his best man. Our front yard was filled with white people, African Americans, Latinos, and people of other ethnicities. It might have looked like a big bowl of gumbo, but we were laughing, dancing, and singing together. It was one of the best days I can remember in my life.

Race is still an issue in America today. We need to get back to loving God and loving each other. Jesus commands us to love one another as He loves us (John 13:34). Our focus doesn't need to be on diversity but on embracing unity. We're all Americans, folks. In the beginning, each of us came from Adam. We're all together as the human race, we're all sinners, and we will all die. However, we can be saved together and get off this earth alive through the death, burial, and resurrection of Jesus Christ. But it will never happen if we don't love each other. Complexion has no bearing on a man's character. It's what's inside a man's heart and soul that matters, not the color of his skin.

8

ENTITLEMENTS

Fix No. 8: Become Self-Reliant

One of the things I've never been able to figure out is why sports fans like to riot after their favorite teams lose. We see it all the time. When an NFL team loses the Super Bowl or a college basketball team falls in the Final Four, a bunch of bad apples will gather in the streets, turn over cars, throw bottles, and act like hooligans. Let me get this straight: a team loses a ball game, and then its fans are ready to tear down the very place where they live? Why do they act this way? Do they actually believe their team was entitled to win the game?

You betcha, Jack. Hey, it's the American way. We are a society without love, a culture without Christ, communities without compassion, streets without self-control, bums with no Bibles, nerds without knowledge, punks without peace, and rebels without reason. We're a sorry lot.

Too many Americans believe they are entitled to money they did not earn. Now, I understand why the government needs to help certain people, like the elderly, children, military veterans, the injured, and the gravely ill. Hey, if you lose your job because of a bad economy, I don't have a problem with the government helping you out until you can find another one. I understand that some people need help learning to stand on their own feet, and that food stamps and assisted housing are sometimes needed for a time. But there is a boatload of Americans who are abusing the system and collecting free money because they're simply too lazy to work. They've become enslaved to this lifestyle and are now entirely dependent on assistance. Why should the hardworking Americans have to pay them to do nothing?

Do you realize how many Americans would react if the U.S. government suddenly declared it was going to stop giving away free money? It would be a free-for-all in the streets! It would be complete chaos. The U.S. government fully understands the chaos that would result if they told the folks who are taking advantage of the system that they weren't entitled to money simply because they're Americans. So the government keeps giving them entitlements like welfare, food stamps, and assisted housing, even when they're fully capable of working. Hey, entitlements are the very reason many of our politicians are even serving in Washington, DC. They promised their constituents that the free money would keep flowing once they were elected, and they certainly can't turn their backs on them after the fact.

I've never figured out why a segment of the U.S. population feels entitled to the wealth of America on the backs of other people's hard work. Just once, I'd love to hear a welfare recipient stand up and say, "You know what? Thank y'all for giving us this money and taking care of our children. We really love y'all because of it." You never hear this kind of thanks because some people actually believe they're entitled to the money. They believe the world owes them something. Hey, news flash: America doesn't owe any of us free money, Jack! When America does give it out, it's a gift—not an entitlement.

In the Declaration of Independence, it says: "We hold these truths to be self-evident, that all men are created equal, that they are endowed by their Creator with certain unalienable Rights, that among these are Life, Liberty and the pursuit of Happiness." Hey, it doesn't say anything about Americans having unalienable rights to receive reduced rent, government-paid cell phones, and free food. I do realize that some people really can't get out and work—for all kinds of different reasons—but a lot of people who are getting this assistance *can* work. To them, I say, get off the couch, go to work, and have a little self-respect. If you're an able-bodied person and the government is sending you free money every month, don't you think it's only fair that you should be out looking for a job, or at least cleaning a park or picking up trash on the side of a highway? It seems to me that you should be doing something productive to repay the free money you receive from someone else.

I've never heard anyone in Washington, DC, acknowledge that the backbone of our country's welfare system is its citizens' concern for our fellow man. Most of the Americans who can afford to pay taxes—the ones who actually pay for entitlements—truly care about the people they're helping. Followers of God understand that He expects us to love and help our neighbors who are in need. That's why we're helping them out. As it says in 1 John 3:17: *"If anyone has material possessions and sees a brother or sister in need but has no pity on them, how can the love of God be in that person?"* God expects us to assist the helpless and needy and that's one of our most important duties as Christians.

> **Most of the Americans who can afford to pay taxes—the ones who actually pay for entitlements—truly care about the people they're helping.**

Since 1964, our federal and state governments have transferred untold trillions of dollars from the middle class and wealthy to the poor. Today, the federal government is spending more than $900 billion annually on Medicare and Medicaid. Half of American households—one out of every two—are receiving some sort of government assistance. Entitlement spending has grown to be almost 100 percent higher than it was in 1960, and the Congressional Budget Office estimates that entitlement spending will consume every federal tax dollar by 2048. Think about that fact, folks. Within thirty-five years, every single dollar the government takes from your paycheck for taxes will go toward non-necessities. It *won't* go toward things like national defense, education, and conservation. Instead, every dollar the government takes in will go toward paying someone else's bills. And we can't figure out why we can't make a dent in the national debt? It's $17 trillion and counting!

The entitlement problem we face in America is cultural. It's really that simple. We have positioned our government as an enabler, and by doing so we've robbed many people of their own sense of personal responsibility. Many Americans are no longer teaching their children the virtues of hard work, self-reliance, and determination. When I grew up, my brothers and I were expected to carry our weight on the family farm. My family didn't have much in terms of material possessions and money, but we earned every single dollar we had. My brothers and I tended to the animals, hoed the fields, and helped our mother in the garden, which supplied the food we ate. Every morning, we milked the cows, fed the animals, and cleaned their pens before going to school. We were dirt-poor, and every one of us pitched in and helped out because we knew we wouldn't eat if we didn't.

Sadly, it's not that way in America anymore. For whatever reason, a growing number of Americans don't believe they have to work. There is a state of mind in this country that makes many of us believe that because we are living on American soil, we are entitled to the American dream without investing anything in it. Many of us believe we are entitled to material things like nice homes, new cars, summer vacations, computers, flat-screen TVs, and cell phones, even if we aren't willing to pour in the blood, sweat, and tears to pay for them. Believe it or not, regardless of what you hear on TV or read on the Internet, we're not even entitled to a college education or job. We have to put in the work and make the necessary decisions to earn a college degree and start a career. We have to work for it.

So how do we fix America's entitlement problem? It's not the government's role to provide charity to its citizens, especially when it requires taking money from other citizens to pay for it.

It's time we get back to the days when we helped and loved one another. The more we do this, the less people would have to count on the government for handouts. When I was in high school in the early 1960s, my father worked as a roughneck, driller, and tool pusher in the oil fields of Louisiana. It was very hard work, but I never heard my pa complain. A short time after we moved to Dixie, Louisiana, Pa fell eighteen feet off the floor of a drilling rig and landed on his head. He was hurt badly and spent the next two years in a neck-to-hip, heavy plaster-of-Paris cast while his broken back healed.

It was a really difficult time for my family. My mother was hospitalized at the time, and Pa received about thirty-five dollars a month in disability payments, which certainly wasn't enough to pay the rent and feed his four children who were still living at home. So my brothers—Tommy and Silas—and I went to work, gathering pecans to sell and cleaning our church building to pay for our school lunches and whatever else we needed. We also received plenty of assistance from our neighbors and friends, includ-

> Back then, neighbors loved each other and wanted to help each other when times were tough.

ing Miss Kay, who brought us food from her parents' grocery. We never asked our neighbors and friends for help, but they believed that helping out a hardworking family in need was the Christian thing to do. My parents knew they could probably never repay the kind folks who helped us, but they were very grateful for their assistance. Back then, neighbors loved each other and wanted to help each other when times were tough.

As I think about the entitlement problem in America, I'm reminded of the Parable of the Workers in the Vineyard in Matthew 20:1–16:

> *"The kingdom of heaven is like a landowner who went out early in the morning to hire workers for his vineyard. He agreed to pay them a denarius for the day and sent them into his vineyard.*
>
> *"About nine in the morning he went out and saw others standing in the marketplace doing nothing. He told them, 'You also go and work in my vineyard, and I will pay you whatever is right.' So they went.*
>
> *"He went out again about noon and about three in the afternoon and did the same thing. About five in the afternoon he went out and found still others standing around.*

He asked them, 'Why have you been standing here all day long doing nothing?'

"'Because no one has hired us,' they answered.

"He said to them, 'You also go and work in my vineyard.'

"When evening came, the owner of the vineyard said to his foreman, 'Call the workers and pay them their wages, beginning with the last ones hired and going on to the first.'

"The workers who were hired about five in the afternoon came and each received a denarius. So when those came who were hired first, they expected to receive more. But each one of them also received a denarius. When they received it, they began to grumble against the landowner. 'These who were hired last worked only one hour,' they said, 'and you have made them equal to us who have borne the burden of the work and the heat of the day.'

"But he answered one of them, 'I am not being unfair to you, friend. Didn't you agree to work for a denarius? Take your pay and go. I want to give the one who was hired last the same as I gave you. Don't I have the right to do what I want with my own money? Or are you envious because I am generous?'

"So the last will be first, and the first will be last."

The vineyard owner told the disgruntled workers, "Look, it's my money, not yours." The situation in this parable is completely different from how the government hands out entitlements. The money they're handing out is *not* their money, and that's why it's so easy to spend. The owner of the vineyard had the right to pay the workers any amount of money he wanted. It was his money. He simply was good to everybody. The workers who'd worked the longest forgot one thing: they agreed to the price they were paid.

But in America nowadays, it's one size fits all because of the entitlement system. Everyone seemingly has a contract with the U.S. government, whether it's for Medicare, Medicaid, or food stamps. But the government doesn't have to help *everyone* who is poor; they could focus their help on the ones in the greatest need—whether it's because they're sick, dying, or disabled. Instead of *always* giving the needy a fish, let's give them a fishing pole. Instead of giving money to everyone who *wants* it, let's only give it to the ones who *need* it. There's a vast difference between those who want and those who are truly in need. Let's put those who can work to work. We shouldn't be enabling people to become completely dependent upon the government; we should be finding them work so they can help themselves. God said if you don't work, you don't eat.

It seems to me that America was better off before welfare even existed, when there was a permeating expectation in this country that you were supposed to work, raise your children, and pay your bills. There's a guy who lives up the road from me who was on welfare and food stamps for a while. He didn't have a job, and he had a wife and children to feed. I'd hired him to do some odd jobs around my property over the years, and I finally asked him, "How am I going to get you off this free government money? What can you do that is constructive?"

"Well, I can drive a truck," he said.

"Okay, here's what I'm going to do," I told him. "I'm going to buy you a truck and a trailer to haul gravel. I'm going to buy you one of those big eighteen-wheelers. It's going to be my truck, but you're going to drive it. You're going to haul gravel, and you're going to haul corn and grain from the farmers' fields. It's going to be a free truck for you to use to earn an honest living. You won't have a truck note, and you won't have to pay for the insurance. I'm going to take care of all of that. Are you with me?"

> "I'm going to buy you a truck and a trailer to haul gravel. It's going to be my truck, but you're going to drive it."

"Keep talking," he said.

"These farmers are going to pay you to haul their corn and grain," I said. "People are going to pay you to bring them gravel. They're going to pay you, and you're going to get to keep that money. You only have to pay for the repairs, gas, and motor oil. Will that get your butt off welfare and food stamps?"

"It sounds too good to be true," he said.

"Well, it is good but it's true," I told him.

I baptized the man in the Ouachita River in front of my house when he was seventeen or eighteen years old. I stayed with him over the years, and I really wanted to get him off the government trough and put him to work. Now he makes an honest living, and I can see that he walks a little taller and has a lot more pride about what he's doing.

There's another young man who works on my land with me. He had struggled with alcohol over the years, but I knew he had a really good heart and loved his wife and kids. About a year ago, a company that builds manufactured houses asked me to do a commercial for them. As part of my compensation, they gave me a new manufactured home they built. They put the double-wide home on a nice part of my property. I decided to let the guy and his family live in it to help them get on their feet.

"If you live your life for Jesus and stay off the bottle, here's what you will get in return," I told him. "You'll get a free double-wide, fully furnished with grass, carpet, and furniture. You get the whole works free of charge, including the insurance. It won't cost you a dime. All of your utility bills will be paid: electricity, water, sewage, everything. All you have to do is move your wife and children into the home, and you'll live happily ever after."

The guy looked at me and grinned, and I knew he thought it was a pretty good deal.

"Oh, it's a good deal," I told him. "I don't know anyone else who is going to make you that kind of deal. Now, your job is going to be to help me around here. That's how I'm going to get repaid. You come out of a farming family. I need help planting the fields with corn, and I want you to sow the land, seed it, and fertilize it every year. I want you to make sure I have a crop over there for ducks. I'm even going to pay you a monthly salary for the work."

Well, the guy and his family moved into the double-wide, and he and his wife cried when they opened the doors for the first time. They're happy, happy, happy. Some of you might be asking, "Why would you do that?" Well, my answer is that's the way America should work. We should individually assist each other. We put people to work and get their labor in return, thereby negating their reliance on the government.

It's a matter of personal responsibility if you ask me. If you're overweight and your blood pressure is shooting through the roof, back away from the table and get some exercise. If you build your house next to the ocean or a river and then a hurricane or flood wipes it out, don't expect the government to come bail you out. When my house was flooded in 1991, we had to replace the flooring and most of the walls because of water damage and mold. It took my boys about three days to get the snakes out of it! But we never received a single dime from the state of Louisiana or the federal government, and we never asked for it. When Miss Kay and I purchased the property, we accepted the risk of the house being flooded. I chose to live here, so it's my responsibility when flooding occurs.

If you build a multimillion-dollar home on the beaches of the Gulf of Mexico, it's going to get blown away by a hurricane one of these days. It's not a matter of if your house is going to get blown over; it's going to get blown away if you live there!

ENTITLEMENTS

You're living on a sandbar next to the ocean. If you look out into the Gulf of Mexico, that's where hurricanes come from. You shouldn't be expecting me, as a citizen of the United States, to be doling out money to you when it happens. You need to move back up the road or back up the hill a little bit. It's about common sense, folks.

Before the federal government started shelling out billions of dollars in federal aid every year, we took care of each other when natural disasters occurred. We have to learn to love each other and take care of each other again. We shouldn't be looking to the states and federal governments to bail us out. If we rely on the government for everything, it will only keep getting bigger and bigger to take care of the 320 million people who are screaming for help every time something bad happens. That's where socialism and communism come from. We look toward the government instead of God, and we don't take personal responsibility for our actions and decisions.

A person who hears Jesus' words and obeys them is the kind of person who built his house on solid ground. Of course, He is the rock, the rock of ages. When the floods come, the man who obeys Jesus' words is up on high ground. He's on rock, so when the winds come, they won't blow his house down. Jesus said a person who does not listen to Him and obey His words is the kind of person who builds his house on sand. When the waters and winds come, his house will be swept away and come down with a crash.

Listen, folks, it's the difference between being wise and fool-ish. The federal government is doling out trillions of dollars in bailouts, whether they're to a failed bank, an automobile manu-facturer, or some guy who pressed his luck by building a house on the sand of the New Jersey shore. They're actually matters of personal responsibility and making the right decisions.

In the autumn of 2013, a couple from New Jersey came to West Monroe, Louisiana, to speak at White's Ferry Road Church. Miss Kay and I sat among the congregation to hear them give their testimonies. The man said that before they turned their lives over to Jesus, they never gave any thought to God. In fact, the man said there wasn't a godly bone in his entire body, not one. He'd never read the Bible and didn't know anything about Jesus Christ.

After the man and woman were married, they built their home on the sands of the Atlantic Ocean. When Hurricane Sandy hit the New Jersey shore in October 2012, the man and his wife decided to ride it out. Hurricane Sandy was so fero-cious that weathermen called it "Superstorm Sandy." It did more than $65 billion damage in the U.S. alone, most of it in New Jersey and New York. There were 115-mph winds com-ing, but it never entered this guy's mind to evacuate! As the night started progressing, the man and his wife sat in their home looking at the ocean, and the water just kept coming. The waves kept getting closer and closer and bigger and big-ger. Eventually, the basement of their home flooded, stuff was banging around and breaking windows, and their washer and dryer floated away.

Well, after the roof of their home was blown off at about three o'clock in the morning, they finally decided it was time to leave the premises! They grabbed their dog and used the top of their carport as a boat. A wave crashed against them, knocking their dog off the metal roof they were floating on. They floated to their neighbors' house, and fortunately the top floor of their home wasn't yet flooded. The man knocked on the door, and their neighbors let them come inside to ride out the storm.

The next day, after the waters of the Atlantic Ocean finally receded, the man and his wife were standing where their house once stood, picking through the debris that was left. The wife told her husband that she couldn't live on the beach anymore because she didn't want to rebuild her life again when another storm came. And she was certain another one would come. She never wanted to walk on the sand or swim in the Atlantic Ocean again.

As they argued, an older man walked up to what was left of their house, and they started sharing their problems with him.

"Well, at a time like this, when it's all gone, you need to hear about somebody maybe you've never heard of," the old man said to them. "You ever heard of Jesus?"

"No, what's He got to do with all of this?" the man asked him.

The older man sat them down and shared what the Bible is about. When he was finished sharing the Good News with them, the man walked the couple into the Atlantic Ocean and baptized them. The woman couldn't believe that she was walking back into the same water that had taken everything from her. Now that water was symbolically cleansing her sins and giving her a new beginning. She was pushed down into the same ocean that had taken everything from her.

After I heard their story, I turned to Miss Kay and told her, "Give those people some money." I told her to give them three hundred dollars, but Miss Kay wrote them a check for a thousand dollars to help them get on their feet again. They didn't come to our church asking for money, but they'd lost everything, and their insurance company turned its back on them. As a Christian and an American, I felt it was my duty to help them out.

I realize not everyone is financially able to put their neighbors to work when they need help, but we could do far more for them than what we're currently doing. We ought to look after each other and love one another the best we can. We need to bring our neighbors to Jesus and help them out. If Americans would begin doing that, instead of relying on the government for handouts, it would be a much better place. It's the right thing to do, and it's what God wants us to do.

> Some of the people we helped slicked us and had ulterior motives, but we never held it against them. You can't let that slow you down.

Miss Kay and I have tried to help as many people as we could over the years. Some of them slicked us and had ulterior motives, but we never held it against them. You can't let that slow you down. You just go forth, and they'll have to answer to God. We've helped more people who appreciated it and benefited from it than those who didn't. I live by a very important code that is found in John 3:16: *"For God so loved the world that he gave his one and only Son, that whoever believes in Him shall not perish but have eternal life."*

Remember, there was a day when welfare and other government assistance programs didn't even exist in America. Families and Christians helped one another. It's not too late to go back there. Governments do not make great individuals, but great individuals make great governments. The answer to our problems is simple: love God and love your neighbors. Will you?

9

---◆◇◆---

GOVERNMENT

Do you know what the United States government and lottery winners have in common? Neither one of them got their money by working for it, both rejoice when the cash pours in, and then both squander it about as fast as they receive it. I've noticed over the years that it's a lot easier to spend somebody else's money than your own because you didn't have to work for it. My boys never had any problems spending my money when they were young. You should try to squeeze a dollar out of them nowadays!

How many stories have we heard or read about lottery winners who strike it big in Powerball or Mega Millions, winning millions of dollars instantly by nothing but dumb luck, only to squander their money on luxurious mansions, extravagant sports cars, and vacations around the world? The money consumes them, and they fall into a life of despair, plagued by sex, drugs, alcohol, and divorce. They're some of the saddest stories you'll ever read because they were ruined by their own greed and, worse, the greed of their families and friends. As the Indian leader Mahatma Gandhi famously said, "Earth provides enough to satisfy every man's need but not for every man's greed." Boy, wasn't he right?

In 1988, William "Bud" Post won $16.2 million in the Pennsylvania Lottery. His brother, of all people, hired a hit man to try to kill him, and Post squandered his fortune in only a few short years. He was living off Social Security when he died in 2006. Billie Bob Harrell Jr. won $31 million in the Texas Lotto in 1997. He divorced his wife and committed suicide less than two years later. Harrell told his financial adviser shortly before his death that winning the lottery was "the worst thing that ever happened to" him. Evelyn Adams, who had the unbelievable fortune of winning the New Jersey Lottery twice, in 1985 and 1986, for a total of $5.4 million, gave away her money and lost the rest gambling in Atlantic City, New Jersey. She was broke and living in a trailer by 2001. I guess what they say is right—money can't buy happiness. But it sure can cause misery.

In many ways, the U.S. government is like a lotto winner who won big—really, really big. The federal government doesn't actually earn its money—it only takes it from you and me—and it has so many methods at its disposal to blow it through fiscal irresponsibility. And like many of the now-broke lottery winners, government officials always seem to say it's someone else's fault when things go wrong. Lottery winners often blame their kinfolk or friends when things go south, and it's always convenient for our politicians to point their fingers at someone else— usually somebody from the other political party—as the reason for their pitiful stewardship.

The U.S. government, as we know it today, is grossly bloated, inefficient, and ineffective at its current size. In 2013, the federal government spent $3.45 trillion while collecting $2.77 trillion in revenues (i.e. taxes), resulting in a deficit of about $680 billion. That probably seems like a pretty big hole, but it was actually an improvement following four consecutive years of trillion-dollar deficits. At the current rate, America is never going to pay off its debt. We're a superpower with a third-world checkbook. We can't even balance it! We owe about $1.3 trillion to China and $1.1 trillion to Japan. How did we become so financially irresponsible and become so indebted to foreign powers? I think it diminishes our standing in the world. As it says in Proverbs 22:7, *"The rich rule over the poor, and the borrower is slave to the lender."* In a word, our government is *greedy*!

The federal government can't slow down when it comes to spending our money. Total U.S. government spending has increased by 40 percent since 2002, even after inflation, and the costs of many mandatory-spending programs (the politicians' fancy term for entitlements) are increasing even more rapidly. Here's the really bad part: it's only going to get worse. Economists predict Obamacare, the federal health care program initiated by President Barack Obama, will add $1.8 trillion to federal health care spending by 2023. So much for what Benjamin Franklin said about a penny saved being a penny earned. Money burns holes in our government's pockets! You know what they say about Washington, DC—it's the only place in the world where your money will leave your pockets faster than it does in Las Vegas.

At its current size, the U.S. government is too big for federal auditors, private citizens, and congressional oversight committees to serve as watchdogs. There is no oversight or accountability when it comes to government spending. If you or I were the CEO of a corporation and operated that way, with so many cost overruns and misallocated funds, our shareholders would run us out of office. If I ran a private business the way we run our government, it would go bankrupt! Duck Commander would have never gotten off the ground if I were so fiscally irresponsible. There is no bottom line in Washington. Our government agencies go on spending sprees at the end of each fiscal year for fear that their budgets will be cut the following year. There's no motivation to save in our government. I guess the American public has become immune to what's going on. When was the last time a politician was run out of office for misspending? It seems the only way a politician loses his or her job anymore is because of a scandalous

> You know what they say about Washington, DC—it's the only place in the world where your money will leave your pockets faster than it does in Las Vegas.

affair. When a politician is caught exposing his private parts via a cell phone, one tends to get a clear picture of why we have ended up where we are as a nation.

If I were ever elected U.S. president—and, hey, you never know—I would slash government agencies by 50 to 75 percent. The current federal government would be a shell of itself by the time I was done. For starters, I would restructure and drastically downsize the Internal Revenue Service, Environmental Protection Agency, Department of the Interior, and the Department of Education. They would be unrecognizable compared to what they are today. I'd put Bibles and prayer back in schools so our children could be taught morals and the difference between right and wrong. I'd return control of the schools back to the states and local communities, where it belongs and can be properly managed. We wouldn't need the EPA because if we learned to love God we wouldn't pollute the earth anymore because He made it. We'd love Him so much we would never destroy His creation.

I'd do away with federal programs in health care, law enforcement, corporate welfare, and foreign aid. I'd eliminate most of the rules and regulations in this country, and we'd learn how to make do with less. I'd do away with welfare and we'd all get back to work. If I were in charge, the federal government would never bail out another corporation again. Hey, suck it up. If you tried something and it didn't work, it's not my job to bail you out. You took the risk, so let it go. I'd get our outsourced jobs back to

America (there were more than 2.6 million U.S. jobs outsourced to foreign countries in 2013)—or the companies doing it would pay severe penalties. Under my watch, we'd quit buying so much of our stuff from China and Japan and take pride in American-made goods again. Consumers would only buy American products, or they'd pay a very hefty price for foreign goods.

Now, to make some serious dents in the federal deficit and make significant changes and reductions in our government, I think you'd have to have a spiritual giant in charge and have the House of Representatives and Senate behind him. The current political ideologies are clashing daily. It's not healthy for anyone.

I understand the war on terror, but do we really have to intercede in every foreign crisis?

Look at the federal government shutdown of 2013. The politicians in Congress couldn't even agree on appropriations bills to fund the government, so they let it shut down for two weeks. It was a complete stalemate, and that's how it's going to continue down the road. The dialogue in Washington needs to change. It needs to become more spiritual as we move ahead. Look, I'm not antigovernment. I'm only saying we need to do some work on our government and the way it operates.

There's certainly plenty to trim in our federal government. Heck, there's less fat on the backside of a Boston butt than there is in Washington. In 2013, there were 2.7 million federal government employees in civilian jobs and another 1.4 million uniformed soldiers in the military. Now, that's actually the lowest number of employees on the U.S. government's payroll since 1966, but you're telling me it can't be cut even more? Hey, I love each and every one of our soldiers, and I certainly appreciate the sacrifices they make for our country, but would our military have to be so big if we kept our nose out of foreign countries' business? I understand the war on terror, but do we really have to intercede in every foreign crisis?

Have you ever seen the list of government agencies? There are more than four hundred and fifty federal agencies, and most of them are divisions in larger agencies' hierarchies. For instance, the U.S. Department of Justice includes eight divisions, six law enforcement agencies, and another twenty-eight offices. In 2012, the U.S. government spent $29 billion on law enforcement and $8.3 billion on federal prisons. Besides counterterrorism and border patrol, law enforcement needs to be handled at the state and local levels. The feds don't need to be policing our communities; we need to be doing it. And guess what? If we learned to love God and love our neighbor, we wouldn't need so much law enforcement policing the streets! The crime rate is always high when the love rate is low.

There is plenty of other wasteful spending in our government. A lot of it leaves me scratching my head. Have you ever heard of the National Wild Horse and Burro Program? You're paying for it. It's part of the U.S. Department of the Interior. How about the Healthy Marriage and

> The crime rate is always high when the love rate is low.

Responsible Fatherhood program? It's part of the U.S. Department of Health and Human Services. You're paying for that, too. But how about pastoring? Why don't we let the churches counsel young couples and newlyweds? The government doesn't need to be doing it. There seems to be a lot of wasted money and manpower in our government.

According to the Cato Institute, a Washington-based think tank, the costs of operating the various federal agencies for each American family are staggering. Their research says the Department of Health and Human Services spent $908 billion in 2013, costing every U.S. household about $7,500. The Social Security Administration spent $873 billion (about $7,300 per household) and the Department of Defense spent $633 billion ($5,200 for every family). Just think if American families could put that money back in their pockets. They could be investing in American-made products and services, and then maybe our economy would turn around. Or, even better, they could be saving their money for financial security in the future. Instead, a lot of the money is being spent to take care of people who don't want to work or given to foreign countries that don't even like us.

If you really want to become angry, take a closer look at how our government is actually spending our money. In 2013, the Interior Department spent nearly $100,000 to install an outhouse on a hiking trail in Alaska. It was an outhouse with one toilet and no internal plumbing! NASA spent nearly $125,000 to try to develop a 3D food printer that would create mini pizzas—I've had more than a few that tasted like cardboard—and the Department of Health and Human Services spent more than $325,000 to fund a study that revealed couples are happier when the woman calms down after an argument. Now, that's groundbreaking stuff! They should have saved their money and called me. My marriage is much happier when Miss Kay isn't bending my ear!

Yep, there's less pork at a Robertson family reunion than what you'll find in Washington. Not surprisingly, the IRS, the very entity that collects our taxes, is one of the most egregious abusers of public money. In 2010, the IRS spent $4.1 million on a lavish conference in Anaheim, California, for more than 2,600 of its employees. The IRS spent $50,000 to produce videos— one of which was a *Star Trek* parody and another of which was line-dancing instruction. Are you kidding me? I'll be sure to write off the ballroom dancing classes Miss Kay makes me go to!

Don't even get me started about the IRS. The U.S. federal tax code would require more than five or six thousand pages of paper to print one copy, and there's no way the average American can figure out what's included in it. It would seem to me that if I'm being taxed by my government, I should at least be able to know why I'm paying it and where my money is going! There has to be a simpler way! I suggest moving Election Day to April 15 every year, so voters would finally hold politicians accountable for their actions. Maybe then our government would realize that there's a serious problem with the way it collects and spends our taxes.

A flat tax would seem to be a much more equitable way of funding our government. It's really a replica of the system of taxation God introduced to us in the Bible. In the Old Testament, tithes were taxes the populace paid to fund Israel's national budget. Many Christians still believe in tithing, which means giving 10 percent of our income to God's work, in and through the ministries of the church. According to Leviticus 27:30–33, *"A tithe of everything from the land, whether grain from the soil or fruit from the trees, belongs to the Lord; it is holy to the Lord. Whoever would redeem any of their tithe must add a fifth of the value to it. Every tithe of the herd and flock—every tenth animal that passes under the shepherd's rod—will be holy to the Lord. No one may pick out the good from the bad or make any substitution. If anyone does make a substitution, both the animal and its substitute become holy and cannot be redeemed."*

Dr. Benjamin Carson of Baltimore, one of the world's most renowned neurosurgeons and a really smart man, suggested a tithing system for taxation during his speech at a National Prayer Breakfast in February 2013. He said it was the most equitable system because it didn't penalize wealthy people for being successful. "You make ten billion dollars, you put in a billion," Carson said at the time. "You make ten dollars, you put in one. Of course, you've got to get rid of the loopholes. . . . Where does it say you've got to hurt the [rich] guy? He just put a billion dollars in the pot. We don't need to hurt him. It's that kind of thinking that has resulted in six hundred and two banks in the Cayman Islands. That money needs to be back here building our infrastructure and creating jobs." I agree with Dr. Carson wholeheartedly. Only 57 percent of American households paid federal income taxes in 2013, and the top 20 percent of wage earners in our country accounted for more than 67 percent of total income taxes, according to some estimates. It isn't fair and it isn't right. Too many hardworking Americans are carrying too much of the weight, and there are far too many freeloaders in our country.

In a lot of ways, we have basically replaced love for God and love for each other with rules and regulations in America. Love trumps all codes, rules, and regulations. Love is the answer. If there's no Jesus, there's no love. Love is a fulfillment of the law. The less love you have, the more laws you will need. That is a fact. We don't love our neighbors anymore, so we try to enforce and legislate everything. But you can't legislate love, you see, because it's something that has to come from the heart.

I still believe America can become the greatest nation on earth again, like it was when our founding fathers established it more than

> The less love you have, the more laws you will need. That is a fact.

two hundred years ago. Our government has simply lost sight of what it's supposed to be and how it's supposed to function. It has become dysfunctional, and it's ripe with greed, corruption, bribery, and deception. But believe it or not, any government is better than no government. Without government, rules, and regulations, there would be anarchy on every level—politically, socially, morally, economically, and domestically. First Peter 2:13–15 tells us we must submit to our government and follow its laws: *"Submit yourselves for the Lord's sake to every human authority: whether to the emperor, as the supreme authority, or to governors, who are sent by him to punish those who do wrong and to commend those who do right. For it is God's will that by doing good you should silence the ignorant talk of foolish people."*

Sadly, faith is no longer important for too many Americans, and so we are no longer under the supervision of God's law. It's a great code of conduct, but unfortunately no one can keep it. Faith in Jesus is the only way out of this thing. We can only pray for our leaders in Washington and hope that God will guide them. As Franklin famously said, "The longer I live, the more convincing proofs I see of this truth, that God governs in the affairs of men. And if a sparrow cannot fall to the ground without His notice, is it probable that an empire can rise without His aid? We have been assured, sir, in the sacred writings, that 'except the Lord build the house, they labour in vain that build it.'"

> **Believe it or not, any government is better than no government. Without government, rules, and regulations, there would be anarchy on every level.**

God wants us to submit ourselves to human authority, but we are to revere no one but God. Why? All men have sinned. God is eternally holy and perfect. He's the only one you revere while you're on planet Earth. Honor those in authority, but don't revere them. More than anything, though, we need to pray for them. Lord knows they sure as heck need it.

10

<hr>

GUN CONTROL

Fix No. 10: Never Give Up Your Firearms

When our founding fathers adopted the Declaration of Independence on July 4, 1776, announcing to the world that the thirteen American colonies had separated from Great Britain to become a new country, the document's preamble introduced a passage that would become the cornerstone for democracy around the world: "We hold these truths to be self-evident, that all men are created equal, that they are endowed by their Creator with certain unalienable Rights, that among these are Life, Liberty and the pursuit of Happiness. That to secure these rights, Governments are instituted among Men, deriving their just powers from the consent of the governed." We best never forget that this republic, America, came into existence because of the Bible, guns, and blood. The blood that spawned our nation came from two sources: Jesus, who died for us, and Americans who bravely gave it to turn away a brutal force, King George and his troops.

According to the Declaration of Independence, I have an unalienable right to the pursuit of happiness, and what makes me happy, happy, happy is blowing a mallard duck's head smooth off. Yes, it is biblically sanctioned by God. Shooting ducks obviously requires me to have a gun, and no one is going to tell me that I don't have an unalienable right to do so, whether it's animal rights groups or gun control advocates. Furthermore, the second amendment to the United States Constitution states: "A well regulated Militia, being necessary to the security of a free State, the right of the people to keep and bear Arms, shall not be infringed." The second amendment was ratified on December 15, 1791, as part of the Bill of Rights, which also protects Americans' freedom of religion, speech, and the press, as well as the right to a fair trial and not having the government unlawfully search and seize your property, among other things.

I've been around guns my entire life and use them to hunt and protect myself. Obviously, people who hunt with guns are the consumers buying my duck calls and other Duck Commander products, so I naturally have a vested interest in the gun debate. It's tragic any time someone dies, either maliciously or accidentally, when a gun is fired. One lost life is one too many. But America doesn't have a gun problem—it has a sin and self-control problem. Guns aren't the problem; it's the people pulling the triggers. The people killing their neighbors and themselves with guns are under the control of the Evil One, along with the terrorists who crash jets into buildings, killing hundreds of people. Trust me, the murder rate in this country would drop dramatically if we started to love God and love one another. It is the solution to all of our country's ailments, as well as the ailments of the entire world. If foreign and domestic terrorists embraced Jesus, our Lord, their murdering would end as well. Satan is leading them—all of them. It is a spiritual problem worldwide. Money and politics are not going to solve our murder problem. Gun control and more rules and regulations are not going to fix it. We're going to have to repent, love God, love our neighbor, and get Jesus back into the equation, and then the murder rate will go down around the world. God doesn't only love America; He loves the whole world.

The arguments for stricter gun laws in this country simply don't add up. According to the Federal Bureau of Investigation's annual uniform crime reports, the nation's total violent crime rate hit an all-time high in 1991. But then it declined in eighteen of the next twenty years, 49 percent overall, to a forty-one-year low in 2011. Forcible rapes were down 36 percent and robberies decreased by 59 percent. At the same time, gun ownership and the number of privately owned guns rose to all-time highs.

> Trust me, the murder rate in this country would drop dramatically if we started to love God and love one another. It is the solution to all of our country's ailments.

In 2012, there were 8,855 homicides committed in the U.S. with firearms, according to the most recent statistics from the U.S. Department of Justice. Another 1,589 people were murdered with knives or cutting instruments. Are we going to ban pocketknives, scissors, and box cutters? An additional 518 people were killed with blunt objects like clubs and hammers. Are we going to take hammers away from carpenters and baseball bats away from kids because some deranged lunatic might use one to beat somebody to death? Is the problem actually the weapons or the hearts of men committing the crimes? The reason people murder is because they don't have a healthy fear of God in their hearts. They don't love God and don't love their neighbor.

Here is an important fact you need to know about gun control: mankind has been murdering for thousands of years. The Law of Moses was introduced around 1500 BC. In the Ten Commandments, God told man, *"You shall not kill."* If God had to instruct people not to murder, they must have been killing each other back then. Firearms weren't invented until the fourteenth century AD, so the Law of Moses was around for at least 2,700 years before guns were introduced. So mankind was murdering with something other than guns. Murder is sin, a violation of the Law. You can't blame sin on the device one uses; you blame the person committing the sin. Where you have no love for Jesus, you have evil and violence. It's as simple as that. Satan has trapped murderers and controls them; he works in them, and he takes them prisoner to do his will. That is why Jesus came to earth—to set us free from Satan. Divine power changes a person's heart. It is the only way to change a heart from hate to love. That's why Jesus is the "the way."

History shows that murder has never been a gun problem. If guns are the problem, then why was there a slaughterhouse happening before guns were invented? People were murdering one another long before pistols and rifles came around. It was never about the weapons. Was it a spear problem when tribes were slaughtering one another? Was it a sword problem back in medieval times? When kings and queens were having public hangings every afternoon at the gallows, was it a rope problem? Would there have been fewer hangings if rope had never been invented? Since the beginning, evil men who did not have love for God and their neighbors killed with spears, rocks, clubs, swords, or anything else they could get their hands on.

It was a love problem when the law was written—do not murder—not a weapons problem. It is a love problem now. We need sin control and self-control. We need a spiritual fix. If you pick any problem plaguing America today, loving God and loving your neighbor are the solutions. If we stop sinning and start doing what's right and loving each other, the murder rate will go down. We need to become spiritual men and women. We need to marry our mates, bring our families back together, and teach our children about fearing God at a very young age so they will love one another and won't shoot each other.

The founding fathers believed every American has a God-given right to liberty and freedom. They also believed every citizen has a right to bear arms to protect themselves and the republic. Samuel Adams, one of the leaders of the American Revolution, said that "the . . . Constitution [shall] never be construed . . . to prevent the people of the United States, who are peaceable citizens, from keeping their own arms." Thomas Jefferson, the third U.S. president, wrote, "No free-man shall ever be debarred the use of arms." He was trying to safeguard our right to keep our guns, and George Washington, the first U.S. president, agreed with him. In Washington's first message to Congress on the State of the Union on January 8, 1790, he said, "A free people ought not only to be armed, but disciplined." Folks, never, ever give up your guns. If you do, you will be at the mercy of the ones you gave them to.

It would seem to me that a criminal intent on robbing a house, raping a woman, or murdering someone would be less inclined to invade a house if he knew the occupants were armed. The only thing that keeps hard-core criminals at bay is not knowing if the people they're about to try to harm are armed. They would be less inclined to come after you if they knew you had guns. It's kind of like somebody saying they're going to stop me on the side of the road and steal

> President Washington said, "A free people ought not only to be armed, but disciplined."

everything from me. I think they're going to leave me alone because they know I'm probably armed—and they would be correct in their assessment.

Unfortunately, evil has reared its ugly head too many times in America. On December 14, 2012, a twenty-year-old man named Adam Lanza murdered twenty elementary school students and six staff members at Sandy Hook Elementary School in Sandy Hook, Connecticut. He killed his mother before attacking the school and then committed suicide when police arrived. It was the second-deadliest mass shooting by a single person in U.S. history, after the 2007 Virginia Tech shooting, in which a student named Seung-Hui Cho killed thirty-two people and wounded seventeen others in two attacks on the campus. On July 20, 2012, a former graduate student named James E. Holmes killed twelve people and wounded seventy others at a movie theater in Aurora, Colorado.

Look, evil people are going to do evil things, whether they have a gun or not. The Evil One has control over them and they're going to kill, whether it's with a high-powered rifle, bomb, knife, or poison. The worst school massacre in U.S. history occurred in Bath Township, Michigan, on May 18, 1927. Andrew Kehoe, a former school board treasurer, detonated two bombs that killed thirty-eight elementary school students and six adults. Kehoe was apparently upset that he'd lost a bid for reelection as town clerk and was losing his family's farm through foreclosure. Remember the 1982 Chicago Tylenol murders?

Someone murdered seven unsuspecting people by poisoning Tylenol capsules with cyanide. What's the weapon of choice for terrorists in the Middle East? They invent ways of doing evil. They use aircraft, suicide bombers, and IEDs to do their carnage. Yeah, they use guns, too.

From the time the U.S. republic was founded, Americans have had a right to protect themselves and their loved ones, and being armed is the best defense against a criminal. Statistics show that people who are carrying guns legally, the ones who go to the local police station or sheriff's office and go through a background check for concealed-carry permits, are far less likely to commit crimes than the general public. It would seem to me that if someone had been armed at the schools or movie theater where the shootings took place, the people who were killed might have had a better chance of survival. The men doing the killing are deranged. America needs to do a better job of punishing violent criminals and getting mental health help to those who need it. The mental health system in this country is an absolute embarrassment.

America needs to do a better job of punishing violent criminals and getting mental health help to those who need it.

We already have gun-control measures in place in this country. Felons aren't allowed to legally own guns. Children can't own guns. It's illegal for parents to leave a loaded gun where a child can find one, and it's illegal to buy a gun for someone who isn't supposed to have one. There are safety training and permit requirements for owners. Have you thought about what our society would be like if Americans couldn't legally own guns? The criminals would be emboldened because they'd know their would-be victims would be unarmed. There are more than three hundred million guns in private hands in our country, according to industry estimates. How would the federal government round them up if they were banned? Would they go door to door, searching everyone's home for guns? It would be illegal and impractical to locate and seize them. The law-abiding citizens, the ones who use guns responsibly, might surrender their guns if it's the law. But the criminals and evil people would only hide them from authorities, creating an environment that would be even worse. It would be utter chaos. It would be complete lawlessness, like it is in places like Afghanistan and Syria. Humanity would turn on itself so fast, and no one would be safe.

It's what happened in a couple of cities that banned its residents from carrying handguns. In 1976, Washington, DC, imposed a law prohibiting its residents from carrying handguns and required all guns in homes to be either unloaded or stored with a trigger lock. By 1991, Washington was the nation's murder capital with 479 murders in one year. The U.S. Supreme Court ruled that Washington's handgun ban was unconstitutional in 2008. In 2012, Washington finished the year with fewer than one hundred murders for the first time since 1963. Likewise, Chicago instituted a handgun ban in 1982, and its murder rate soared to 936 deaths in 1992. Chicago's gun ban was invalidated by a U.S. circuit court of appeals in 2010.

Stricter gun-control laws won't work because criminals will still find ways to get their hands on guns illegally, and law-abiding citizens will be left defenseless. Look what happened during Prohibition in the 1920s and 1930s—no one stopped drinking and crime only got worse.

Statistics show that limiting the populace's access to guns won't necessarily cause murder rates to decline. In 1960, there were about 4.3 guns for every ten Americans. The number of murders by firearms was 5.1 per one hundred thousand residents. It is estimated that there are now 310 million firearms in America—more than there are actual citizens—and there were 3.6 murders by firearms per one hundred thousand residents in 2010, according to the most recent statistics compiled by the Centers for Disease Control. So even though the number of guns in America more than quadrupled, the murder rate declined.

I have to admit that I do find it remarkably ironic that many of the people who want to control guns are also pro-choice advocates when it comes to abortion. Many of the same people who want to rid the U.S. of guns are advocating for the murder of millions of babies. It's pretty incredible to me that in one breath they're advocating for abortion, while in the next breath they're saying, "Boy, if we could just do something about these guns, think about how the murder rate would go down." It's absolute nonsense. In 2010, there were more than seven hundred thousand abortions performed at clinics that report to the CDC. A report published by the National Right to Life Committee in 2011 estimated there were more than 54 million abortions performed in America since the U.S. Supreme Court handed down its 1973 *Roe v. Wade* ruling. We have lost more Americans to murder through abortion than through all the wars we have ever fought. It's embarrassing and a terrible blight on all of us. Fortunately, the blood of Jesus is more than sufficient to forgive those who have committed the act.

As I wrote in my first book, it's amazing to me that it's more difficult to kill a duck in this country than it is to rip an unborn child out of its mother's womb. Where I live in eastern Louisiana, I can hunt only sixty days each year. The government tells me how many ducks I can kill, and I can shoot only so many of each species. I can kill six ducks per day, but I can never be in possession of more than twelve ducks at once. We're talking about ducks. Abortion clinics are open year-round, some of them six days a week. It's open season on babies. The financial cost of an abortion averages somewhere between $430 and $1,500, depending on at what point in the pregnancy it occurs. In California, nurse-practitioners, nurse-midwives, and physician assistants can even perform early abortions now. You don't even have to be a doctor to do it. It's that easy—and it's criminal.

> Abortion clinics are open year-round, some of them six days a week. It's open season on babies.

One of the big questions in the abortion debate revolves around the viability of a fetus to survive outside of its mother's womb. Science has determined for years that a new individual human being begins at fertilization, when the sperm and ovum meet to form a single cell. Psalm 139:13 tells us: *"For you created my inmost being; you knit me together in my mother's womb."* What the pro-choice advocates are really doing is trying to play God to determine when a baby has a life of its own. Some people suggest a fetus isn't viable at nineteen weeks, but that it is at twenty-two weeks and shouldn't be aborted then. Are you kidding me? You're going to decide whether to abort a baby based on three weeks' time? That is brutality. It is heartless, faithless, and senseless.

One of the definitions of *viable* in *Merriam-Webster's Dictionary* is: "capable of living or of developing into a living thing." I know this sounds weird, America, but is *sin* still in the dictionary? Ask your mother when she knew she was pregnant with you. She's going to tell you, "I knew it was you the entire time," because she's a mother. God knows us before He forms us in the womb. As it says in Jeremiah 1:5: *"Before I formed you in the womb I knew you, before you were born I set you apart; I appointed you as a prophet to the nations."* The doctors, legislators, and judges are trying to put themselves in God's shoes and decide who's going to live.

It's spiritual warfare. We need to turn our country around, but only time will tell. In the meantime, we have to love them, instruct them, show them the way, show them the truth, show them the life, show them the resurrection, show them Jesus, and pray for them. They're being led down a road they should not travel by the depraved. They're like sheep without a shepherd. They've gone astray, so we must show them and tell them the Good News.

PART THREE

FAITH

11

INTELLIGENT DESIGN OR BLIND CHANCE

Fix No. 11: Look at Creation, You'll Figure It Out

Have you ever looked closely at a watermelon seed? It's black, flat, and weighs nearly nothing. You could easily hold one on the tip of your finger. But if you throw a watermelon seed into sandy dirt and water it a few times each week, it's truly amazing what happens next. The first thing you'll see is a vine running across the ground. Then you'll start to see flowers with swollen buds, and before too long you'll begin to see round melons that will eventually multiply in weight five thousand times over what the seed weighed. When the watermelon becomes ripe and you bust it open, its skin is green, its rind is usually pale green or white, and its flesh is the prettiest red you'll ever see. Now ask yourself: *How did all that color come from a tiny black seed?*

And what about acorns? You don't even have to plant them. They fall to the ground from oak trees, and a new oak tree will actually sprout from the ground where the acorn was. That tree will grow to be fifty feet tall and live for hundreds of years. The acorn weighs less than an ounce, but it turns into something that weighs tons. If you cut down an oak tree, its wood is so strong and durable that you can use it to build a house or furniture. And it came from that tiny acorn that fell to the ground. Now ask yourself: *How did something that small grow to become something so big?*

How does a tiny seed turn into a watermelon or an acorn into an oak tree? There's only one conclusion—there is tremendous power at work to make it happen. Humans can't do that. We can't touch it. This amazing transformation is living proof of the resurrection. Something dies (totally ceases to be what it was) when it goes into the ground, and we simply watch what happens next. Every day we witness the resurrection of living things all around us. The fact that something so small as acorns and watermelon seeds ends up growing into something so big defies all logic.

Everything we see around us in nature points to God's majesty and breathtaking creative ability. Only God can create something out of nothing. We know He's here based on what He has made (that's the assertion made in Romans 1:20). Based on just a paltry look at two examples out of literally millions that could be made, I'm convinced the only explanation for the cause of the world in which we live is an all-powerful, all-present, all-knowing, and loving God.

Another example? Look closely at the honeycomb. It is made of rows and rows of individual cells that are the perfect shape of a hexagon. What's so special about that? Engineers will tell you that the hexagon is a strong, rigid shape, capable of holding much weight. So how did the honeybee know to build its comb out of hexagons instead of squares, rectangles, or triangles—which would have collapsed under the weight of honey? Hey, have you ever looked at a honeybee's head? It's all eyes—there's not a lot of room in there for brains.

The fossil evidence shows that hexagonal structures have always been used for honeycombs. Honeybees arrived on earth knowing they had to build their honeycombs into hexagons. People call it "instinct" when an insect or fish or animal does something naturally that it obviously cannot think through or reason out. I call that internal design—and it's everywhere. The Creator put it in them; it's not there by "chance."

Back when I was attending college at Louisiana Tech University in Ruston, Louisiana, during the late 1960s, my college professors told me that in the beginning humankind "crawled out of the ocean." I was only eighteen years old, but I scratched my head and thought, *Hmmm, I don't know about that.* The evolutionists deliberately forget that long ago, according to Scripture, the heavens existed and the earth was formed "out of water and by water" (2 Peter 3:5). The evolutionists at least know there was a lot of water here, but unfortunately for them, they don't include God in the mix. To this day, there's no known process, working model, or theory on *how* living things can be created from only water. There has to be a Designer. "Chance" simply cannot make something as complex as a living cell with its untold tens of thousands of coordinated chemical reactions, including the construction of its DNA. Every biochemist knows this. Yes, they theorize that "given enough time, everything is possible." I say that's not very satisfying science.

When I look at our galaxy, our solar system, and Earth, the sun, and the moon—and all their interaction with and dependence on each other—it's impossible for me to believe this all happened by chance. I have to believe there's intelligent design behind it all. Billions of galaxies fill the universe, and those galaxies contain billions of stars rotating around an axis. It's really overwhelming when you look at the nighttime sky and ponder it all. And then on the opposite end of the scale, you have watermelon seeds, acorns, and honeycombs. Wow! There's a great power on display, and that power should be honored.

> To this day, there's no known process, working model, or theory on *how* living things can be created from only water. There has to be a Designer.

It's all from either total chance or purposeful design. Think about it. Putting an oak tree inside an acorn? With all the life cycle built in, the design for leaves, the DNA to direct the photosynthetic process, and the vascular tissue to transport fluids throughout the tree? Then there's the fact that trees give off oxygen for us to breathe, and they provide us with wood. Are you kidding?

Some have argued that it's "unscientific" to suggest that intelligent design is present. Really? So what's so "scientific" about saying it all happened by chance? In all of human history we've never seen any complex functioning entity that was created by swishing water or a windstorm. A house has a complex design. A TV has a complex design. A saltshaker or duck call has a design. Even something as simple as a golf tee was designed! Look at the spiral helix construction of a DNA molecule and tell me that's not design! Look at your eye! Good grief, Jack! It screams design! Design by definition is the result of planning—the opposite of chance. And I see design in every aspect of creation, right down to the atom, for crying out loud!

The first words of the Bible in Genesis 1:1–2 are as follows: *"In the beginning God created the heavens and the earth. Now the earth was formless and empty, darkness was over the surface of the deep, and the Spirit of God was hovering over the waters."* That's the first statement in Scripture. It's either true or false. I believe it to be true. I believe the Bible is a historical narrative given by the infallible Creator to humanity. In many ways, the Bible is a love letter to humankind, and it explains the reality in which we live. The answer to every question in life is found in the Bible.

And then there's the question of how much time passed in verses one and two. It says "created" and "was hovering." Those words indicate action and time but don't say how much. Was it an instant? Maybe. Or was the amount of time much longer? Possibly. I think people make a mistake when they make the Bible say things it doesn't say. We do not know how much time the process of the creation of matter took in verse one. The Bible doesn't say. Genesis 1:1–2 is not dated. The days of Genesis 1, whatever they were, had not yet started. So I'm leaving it at that. Time means nothing to an infinite God who is not constrained by time. We've made many assumptions about the amount of time the creation took, but we don't know for sure, so let's not yell at each other about it. The primary message of Genesis chapter 1 is not "how long" or "when." It's *"what"* and *"Who."* "What" is that this all has a beginning, and "Who" is God, the Creator.

The opening statement in the Bible is about the creation of matter. That's the first big problem the atheists and secularists have. They can't explain the origin of matter. There is no physical cause to explain it. Yet, we know that something does not come from nothing. (And don't jump into quantum mechanics or strings or other dimensions. Those are all still a something.)

Secular scientists pretty much assert that the universe is fourteen or fifteen billion years old. They say this because the universe is observed to be rapidly moving apart. Envision a ripple on a pond. When you see the ever-widening circles from a ripple, you know that moments before some event caused the ripple. Based on the distance of the ripples and the rate of their expansion, you can approximate when the event happened. That's what the "Big Bang" theory is all about. Matter—the galaxies—is moving apart at a very rapid speed. So some time in the past, something very dramatic happened. Boom! A couple of questions are obvious. What blew up? And where did it come from? Science can't answer that. But it is obvious there was a "First Cause."

Here's the catch. Matter cannot make itself from nothing. You can throw out theories all day, but in the end the bottom line is that there is no physical process by which matter can come from absolutely nothing. That would violate the laws of physics we use every day. The infinitely teeny speck of a proton or singularity that expanded (causing the Big Bang) is still something. The Big Bang does not explain the First Cause. Who or what made it? The laws of physics do not preclude a nonphysical entity—an entity not bound by the laws of physics—from operating. That, my friend, is God—a spiritual, nonphysical entity not bound by the laws of physics, Who operates in ways we cannot comprehend—the Creator.

On the first day, God created light. Scholars will tell you that the Hebrew word for *day* that was used in the original text means a period of time. It can mean a day as we know it or it can mean an indefinite period of time. That's not the issue I'm discussing. I'm discussing a chronological order that we observe in the record of the earth. And it was very orderly and logical.

Genesis 1:3–5 says, *"And God said, 'Let there be light,' and there was light. God saw that the light was good, and he separated the light from the darkness. God called the light 'day,' and the dark-ness he called 'night.' And there was evening, and there was morn-ing—the first day."* God called the light "day," and we still call it that, and He called the darkness "night," and we still call it that. We still refer to the start of light each day as "morning" and the beginning of darkness each day as "evening."

On the second day, God created the sky. According to Gen-esis 1:6–8, *"God said, 'Let there be a vault [expanse] between the waters to separate water from water.' So God made the vault and separated the water under the vault from the water above it. And it was so. God called the vault 'sky.' And there was evening, and there was morning—the second day."*

On the third day, according to Genesis 1:9–10, God said, *"'Let the water under the sky be gathered to one place, and let dry ground appear.' And it was so. God called the dry ground 'land,' and the gathered waters he called 'seas.' And God saw that it was good."*

So in the beginning Earth was a big ball of water, and then here comes the ground. The land comes out of the water, and the sky is lifted above the seas. For my money, it could not have happened without a Guiding Hand!

There is an extreme amount of scientific evidence to indi-cate that water covered Earth several billion years ago (as sci-entists date it). The continents didn't exist, and scientists say there was a big mass of water that covered the surface of the Earth. When you're flying in a jet over Arizona, you can look down out your window and see evidence that water covered the desert a long time ago. There are sediment layers visible on the walls of canyons and deep trenches that were caused by the presence of a sea that was there at one time. We've discovered fossils of fish and other sea creatures in the rocks of the Grand Canyon and other locations. It's a desert now, but there's plenty of evidence that there was a lot of water there at one time.

The Spirit of God was hovering, and He waited until the planet was right to introduce life. He waited for the correct rotation of Earth, the correct distance of Earth from the sun and moon. We all know that the distance of Earth from the sun just "happens" to be the right distance for water to remain a liquid as needed and for our climate to be livable. If the sun were too close, we'd burn up; a little farther out, and we'd freeze. It's just right. Not only is the distance precise, but the ratio of land to water is critical for the planet's temperature balance to work (land and water absorb and release heat at different rates, so the ratio of land to water is extremely important). And there's more. Where the continents are located is also critical. The Northern Hemisphere has more land than the Southern Hemisphere, and that is important to the global temperature. And then there's the spin rate—critical again. Oh yeah, there's the tilt of our axis at 23.5 degrees off the vertical. Critical. So you see, there are many design features that have to all happen on the right planet at the right distance from the sun for our temperatures and weather to balance. I see a lot of design! Don't you?

When the time was right, God introduced plants and animals to Earth and then humans—in that order. Genesis 1:11–13 says, *"Then God said, 'Let the land produce vegetation: seed-bearing plants and trees on the land that bear fruit with seed in it, according to their various kinds.' And it was so. The land produced vegetation: plants bearing seed according to their kinds and trees bearing fruit with seed in it according to their kinds. And God saw that it was good. And there was evening, and there was morning—the third day."* God created the vegetation because the animals and humans were to follow and would need something to eat. I guess that's something the evolutionists forgot. They believe everything came from water, and that's why they're looking for water on Mars. What it boils down to is that they believe elephants came out of water. They think trees came out of water. They contend bugs did, too. They believe you and I emerged from the water—everything made via chemical reactions by blind chance. Blind is right!

Well, let me ask you something: By what process can human flesh come out of salt water? We just crawled out of the salt water? Oh, really? Now, I'm not a rocket scientist. I'm more of a C+ man. Half of the American population is smarter than I am (at least I'm smarter than the other half), but I don't think water can pull it off. Raccoons and ducks and palm trees from blind chance working with salt water to make all this? Not hardly!

Where did apples come from? Plums? Did corn, wheat, barley, cucumbers, persimmons, tomatoes, nuts—each with their own DNA codes—all come from salt water? Don't put your faith in that! The narrative of the Bible is that God prepared the planet for animal and human life, and then salad (vegetation) was the first item on the menu to sustain them. Logical. Exactly what you would expect from an intelligent Being.

Evolutionists propose, basically, that before we were humans, we were apes; and before that, rats; and before that, lizards; and before that, salamanders; and before that, fish; and so on, all the way back to the protozoans. Give me a break! So they're saying that now we're catching, battering, frying, and eating what we used to be? I don't think so.

Before a cell divides, DNA determines what it's going to be. The DNA code is very stable. DNA is not random. I have my DNA, and you have yours. Dogs have theirs, and cats have theirs, toads have theirs, and it's stable in kind after kind. Every living kind of plant and animal has its own distinctive, stable DNA code. The blind-chance-one-cell-mutation-eventually-to-man theory doesn't work. It's a theory with large assumptions and missing tens of millions of "intermediate" forms in the fossil record (a problem Darwin recognized). That dog won't hunt.

> So they're saying that now we're catching, battering, frying, and eating what we used to be? I don't think so.

Evolutionists tell us that every single living thing on Earth came from the same bowl of soup. But the hard science, the fossil record of all those intermediates mutating and changing, is just not there. Every class of animal, bird, reptile, fish, invertebrate, and so on that we find in the fossil record is fully formed with its characteristics the first time it appears in the fossil record. (Evolutionists know this, by the way.)

Certainly, there has been adaptation and limited evolution, or change, among the various types of living organisms through time. Noah did not have four hundred different species of dogs on the ark. He had representatives of different kinds of animals—not each individual species. There are breeds of dogs, hogs, various crops, etc., living today that did not exist even one hundred years ago. Living things are adaptable—and they change—but it's "kind after kind" (Bible terminology). Living organisms can adapt as the climate or conditions change. Look at Darwin's finches for example—different kinds of beaks. But they were all finches, and they never became another kind of organism! Horses have evolved from smaller forms in their early history to larger animals today. But they were all the same kind of creature—horses. They did not become hippos, giraffes, or lions.

Over the years, evolutionists have taken a lot of liberties with their theories, and they can always find a way to get theoretical assertions printed in various magazines and schoolbooks, on TV, and so on. They would have the public believe it's all been worked out as established science. Hogwash! Never has so much theory been sold as so much fact with so little real evidence as in the case of the evolution-as-explanation-for-all-life idea. It simply does not account for all the diverse, highly complex, and unique forms of life that have lived. Bottom line, the intermediates theorized are not there.

Consider the following—a simple birdhouse, a doghouse, your house, a grand hotel. They all have certain things in common—walls, an entrance, a roof, and other touches. Why do they have a similar pattern? We attribute it to intelligence—ours. We take a functional design and then adapt it to whatever purpose we have for it. Isn't that exactly what we expect from an intelligent Designer?

Look at a whale's flipper, a duck's wing, a squirrel's front leg, and your arm. They all have a large bone above the hinge (elbow) and a couple of smaller bones below the hinge, and then several smaller bones (phalanges) at the end. Science says these indicate a "common origin." I say "yes, they do"—but was it blind chance or intelligence? Take a functional design, and then adapt it to whatever purpose it serves. Again, that's exactly what we would expect from an intelligent Designer.

There is no rule that says we have to accept blind chance, whether wind, explosion, or wave action (these forces never organize systems), as the only possible organizer of cells, DNA, protein synthesis, the nervous system, bone tissue, the endocrine system, the autoimmune system, the respiration process, and so on. To say it was by blind chance takes an awful lot of faith!

Those who defend the religion of blind chance often do so by intimidating, belittling, criticizing, yelling, and bullying those with other views (why are they so defensive?). All the while, they can't show the working model or pathways that demonstrate how the creation of life, a living cell, occurred—just a fervently held faith that we could not have come from an intelligent Designer. Their faith, secular evolution, provides no reason or purpose for your existence now, and no hope for the future. Pride and resistance to the concept of a Creator (to whom we are obliged) is a powerful emotional response that ignores a logical option to "chance." Intelligence. I'm telling you, don't ever doubt that you have a purpose, because you were made on purpose!

The origin of matter, the atom, Earth, the chemical processes by which DNA was formed, life, and on and on—you can find the theories. But they are only theories with no real answers. In the end, you put your faith in either blind chance or an intelligent Being. I find the latter much more satisfying and reasonable.

Back to the biblical account: After God introduced vegetation, He created the sun and the moon on the fourth day and said, *"Let there be lights in the vault of the sky to separate the day from the night, and let them serve as signs to mark sacred times, and days and years, and let them be lights in the vault of the sky to give light on the earth"* (Genesis 1:14–15). Did you notice that using the sun to count days and time, as we do now, is not introduced until verses fourteen and fifteen, on the fourth day? So God created light on the first day (verse three) but did not localize that light into the sun to count days and seasons until much later.

The vegetation created on the third day had light (verse three), but the sun as we know it was not formed until the fourth day.

Genesis 1:20 tells us that on the fifth day, *"God said, 'Let the water teem with living creatures, and let birds fly above the earth across the vault of the sky.'"* The fish are in place, and then come the birds, which feed on the fish and vegetation. The water was "teeming" with living things—from microscopic to bigger and bigger—a food chain. To this day, you can go to the ocean and see shrimp, shad, mackerel, albacore tuna, swordfish, and sharks all still according to their "kind." What about the winged creatures? There are robins, bluebirds, sparrows, owls, hawks, and eagles. There are mallard ducks, teal ducks, wood ducks, and gadwalls. All covered in feathers with unique and beautiful markings. And they're all reproducing kind after kind.

Genesis 1:24 says, *"And God said, 'Let the land produce living creatures according to their kinds: the livestock, the creatures that move along the ground, and the wild animals, each according to its kind.'"* The earth was created for humankind to inhabit. Living creatures were placed here before we were. We needed a food supply: vegetation, fish, birds, and wild animals—they were all created for us. And God gave us permission to whack 'em and stack 'em.

According to Genesis 1:26–28, *"God said, 'Let us make mankind in our image, in our likeness, so that they may rule over the fish in the sea and the birds in the sky, over the livestock and all the wild animals, and over all the creatures that move along the ground.' So God created mankind in his own image, in the image of God he created them; male and female he created them."* He introduced Adam and Eve to Earth and all that he had created for them.

God wanted people to rule over the fish in the sea and the birds in the sky. There are your ducks, geese, quails, and pheasants. God wanted people to rule over the livestock and wild animals. There are your four-footers like deer, bears, moose, and squirrels. He told us everything that lives and moves would be food for us. So much for PETA and these other animal rights groups telling me I shouldn't be shooting ducks. God sanctioned me to do it, Jack!

One word here about people being made in God's image. What makes us human? It's not intelligence. It's not standing on two legs. It's our soul and spirit made in God's image. The existence of a conscience, moral values (when man doesn't smother it because of sin), ethics, aesthetics, and abstract qualities are all *spiritual* qualities. These qualities do not come from dirt or water; they are not found in the animal kingdom. They come from God. Spiritual qualities exist today because they were part of the "First Cause," God, in the beginning.

Based on what I've read in the Bible and what I've seen on earth, I know there will be a resurrection of human bodies from the ground. I see resurrection all around me. The secular crowd and many evolutionists say they don't believe in God. They ignore what He gave us. When, in fact, we should be in awe of what God gave us. It is literally amazing. He can grow a plant from a seed the size of a grain of rice and make a bull redwood out of it that would take several trucks and loaders to haul off. Everywhere I look in nature, I see evidence of a Designer.

I can't measure God or weigh Him to prove Him to you in a physical sense. And our secular friends cannot prove that He is not there. He operates in another dimension (as well as this one). He is Spirit. I choose to accept by faith (and by looking at a lot of evidence) that He is here! I look at what has been made, and it screams "intelligent design" to me from every direction. I didn't major in biology or chemistry. I'm an average-intelligence guy. I also know that the chair you're sitting in right now did not just fall into place. It was thought about. Then it was constructed. It's design.

Scientists have used this same logic. You've heard of the SETI (Search for Extraterrestrial Intelligence) project. How are they going to determine if space aliens are out there? They are searching for radio waves—a pattern of radio pulse. In other words, they are looking for intelligent design in the form of radio waves or Morse code or the like. It makes no sense that secular people rant about intelligent design not being scientific. It's the very principle the SETI scientists have been using since the 1980s. And then there's the science of archaeology. Archaeologists search through dirt and make determinations about past peoples when they discover some drawing or artifact that shows what? Intelligent design.

A scientist you've all heard of, Albert Einstein, once said, "Try and penetrate with our limited means the secrets of nature and you will find that, behind all the discernible laws and connections, there remains something subtle, intangible, and inexplicable. Veneration for this force beyond anything that we can comprehend is my religion. To that extent I am, in fact, religious."

I've read the Bible from cover to cover many times in my life, and I can't get over the fact that fifty or so individuals, who were scattered out across the world and whose lives were spread out thousands of years apart, each picked up where the last one left off and continued a story that is the answer to our existence on earth. On their own, that many people, separated by time and distance, could not create a story beginning with the creation of the cosmos and moving to the end. And then they weaved into it the prophecies to be fulfilled by one Man—seeing His birth, His death to remove our sin, His resurrection from the grave, and the contentment of a godly life and all that's involved in an eternal inheritance. I believe God was speaking through them. It was His plan. Such a story over time is beyond man's capacity to contrive. The Bible has to be true. It is the story of all time, and it is for us!

Every time I look around me, I see His creation. There is no other explanation for watermelons and acorns and honeycombs.

> Such a story over time is beyond man's capacity to contrive. The Bible has to be true. It is the story of all time.

I also know Jesus Christ was here and is the Son of God. We are still counting time by Him! He died to pay my sin penalty. He was buried, and He was raised from the dead to show me I can be raised, too. God has defeated death for us. These facts give me faith that there is an eternal future and that I can get off the planet alive.

12

---※◆※---

GOOD VS. EVIL

Fix No. 12: Choose to Live Righteously

Some of my favorite movies had classic story lines of good versus evil. Let's face it: the heart of every good story is a struggle, and oftentimes it's a hero against a villain. Who will ever forget Rocky Balboa fighting Apollo Creed and Ivan Drago in the *Rocky* movies or Jake La Motta battling Ray Robinson in *Raging Bull*? Hey, my all-time favorite actor is Clint Eastwood, who battled serial killers and hit men as the protagonist in the *Dirty Harry* movies. "Go ahead, make my day," Eastwood told them. No matter the odds, we always seem to find ourselves rooting for the underdog, the outnumbered, and the outsized.

Let me tell you something, folks: we're facing that kind of struggle in America every day. In my sixty-seven years on earth, I've learned that I'm coexisting with two kinds of people: good ones and evil ones. I'm only talking about the creatures living on earth because that's where I happen to reside. It's actually a much bigger battleground, but we'll start with planet Earth for now. According to 1 John 5:19, *"We know that we are children of God, and that the whole world is under the control of the evil one."* In case you haven't figured it out yet, let me reveal this startling fact: there are far fewer children of God on earth than there are people being controlled by the evil one. We're the underdogs, the outnumbered and outsized.

Now, I know that's a mouthful and a big pill to swallow. But when you think about the world today, that particular scripture from the Bible explains why everything happens the way it does. Understanding that the world is under the control of the Evil One explains killing, wars, robberies, injustices, and why men do what they do. It explains why a group of men would get on four jet airplanes on the morning of September 11, 2001, and fly the jets into tall buildings full of people in New York and Washington, DC. Hey, let me get this right: The terrorists didn't know the passengers on the airplanes and didn't know the people in the buildings. They'd never met them. You had women and children in the mix, but the terrorists still hijacked the planes with smiles on their faces and rammed them into the World Trade Center towers and the Pentagon, killing nearly three thousand people in an instant.

If you're anything like me, you probably asked yourself on 9/11: *What in the world were they thinking?* They weren't thinking for themselves, folks. They were under the control of the Evil One. It explains why they did what they did. I know that's probably enough to make you say, "Good grief!" But I'm only getting started, and it's going to become crystal clear as you read this.

Look at what two brothers did during the Boston Marathon on April 15, 2013. It was a foot race with thousands of people running in the streets of Boston. It's an American tradition and a celebration of Patriots' Day, which commemorates the battles of Lexington and Concord in Massachusetts, the first military engagements of the American Revolutionary War. But as the people of Boston celebrated on what was a beautiful spring day, two brothers carried two pressure-cooker bombs in their backpacks and placed them near the finish line of the race. When the brothers set them down, there were women and children everywhere. The brothers walked about fifty yards away, looked at their cell phones, and then consciously and knowingly punched in a code to detonate the bombs and blew the legs off women and children. The bombings killed three people and injured more than two hundred and fifty others.

The terrorists who attacked Boston lived in America, after fleeing the former Soviet Union and immigrating to the U.S. They were college students. Why would they do something evil like that to their fellow countrymen? Why did they hate us? You're probably asking yourself: *What in the world were they thinking?* They were under the control of the Evil One; that's why they did it.

In today's world, our children are being taught that there are no such things as good and evil, and they're being told that it is wrong to suggest that something is good or evil. When Adam and Eve were first created, they weren't expected to know the difference between good and evil. It wasn't until after they ate from the tree of knowledge of good and evil that they understood the difference. The fruits of the trees weren't evil; it was the disobedience of Adam and Eve—who had been told by God not to eat the fruits—that was evil. We inherently understand the difference between good and evil—even without being taught. Remember the Golden Rule? Whatever you want someone to do for you, do that for them. We are born knowing what we want done to us; that's how we know what's good and evil.

The Scripture tells us that there is an absolute truth. John 17:17 says that God's Word is truth, and John 8:44 reveals that the devil is a *"liar and the father of lies."* God's words are not just temporary truths; they're eternal and always true. The Bible is full of words like *good, evil, sin,* and *wicked.* The Scripture tells us time and time again to embrace things that are good and shun things that are evil. And if we don't reject evil, we'll face God's wrath. The only way out of our entrapment is through the blood and grace of Jesus Christ. None of us can live the perfect life—but we can get out from under the control

> **We inherently understand the difference between good and evil—even without being taught.**

of the Evil One. That's what Jesus offers, and that's what I'm talking about.

There's no doubt in my mind that the Evil One exists. If you know anything about my story, I spent the first twenty-eight years of my life living among the sinners. I was an alcoholic and was consumed by my desires for immorality and lawlessness. I even kicked my wife, Miss Kay, and our three young boys out of our home for a while. There's no doubt about it: I was among the disobedient and I was controlled by the Evil One until I was called to follow God and lead a life of faith.

This description in the book of Ephesians is talking about me:

> *As for you, you were dead in your transgressions and sins, in which you used to live when you followed the ways of this world and of the ruler of the kingdom of the air, the spirit who is now at work in those who are disobedient. All of us also lived among them at one time, gratifying the cravings of our flesh and following its desires and thoughts. Like the rest, we were by nature deserving of wrath.* (Ephesians 2:1–3)

Paul the Apostle was writing to a group of people who had gotten out from under the control of the Evil One. He was talking about people like me.

Galatians 3:22 tells us that the whole world is a prisoner of sin. Let's see: the Evil One is controlling, he's working in them, and he literally has imprisoned them. That's a pretty good bind to be in, don't you think? I was once dead in the eyes of the Lord. I was controlled by the Evil One and was among his prisoners. But God used his servants to "gently instruct" me in the Good News of Jesus, and God granted me repentance—as Timothy explains: *"The Lord's servant must not be quarrelsome but must be kind to everyone, able to teach, not resentful. Opponents must be gently instructed, in the hope that God will grant them repentance, leading them to a knowledge of the truth,"* (2 Timothy 2:24-25).

Yes, God will grant the disobedient repentance, but I'm showing you where most of the world is right now. Paul's description in Ephesians 2 is an indictment of America. You've probably heard this phrase your entire life: *You will know the truth and the truth will set you free.* Well, now you know from whom you are being set free. If the Evil One has someone under his control and is causing them to be disobedient, then he has imprisoned them. But there is hope, and that hope comes through hearing the message of Jesus.

In Acts 26, Jesus personally took his message to a known murderer. The murderer's name was Saul of Tarsus, who was later renamed Paul the Apostle. Saul of Tarsus led a life of great wickedness; he was a persecutor, a blasphemer, an injurer, an unbeliever, and the chief of sinners—according to 1 Timothy 1:12–15. Saul was dragging Christians out of their homes in Jerusalem and having them stoned to death. That's what he did for a living! He was killing the people of God. Is that still going on today? Yeah, it still happens today.

As Saul of Tarsus made his way to Damascus, a brilliant light from heaven shone upon him and struck him to the ground. Saul then heard a voice demanding to know why he was persecuting the Man behind the voice. As it says in Acts 26:14–18:

We all fell to the ground, and I heard a voice saying to me in Aramaic, "Saul, Saul, why do you persecute me? It is hard for you to kick against the goads."

Then I asked, "Who are you, Lord?"

"I am Jesus, whom you are persecuting," the Lord replied. "Now get up and stand on your feet. I have appeared to you to appoint you as a servant and as a witness of what you have seen and will see of me. I will rescue you from your own people and from the Gentiles. I am sending you to them to open their eyes and turn them from darkness to light, and from the power of Satan to God, so that they may receive forgiveness of sins and a place among those who are sanctified by faith in me."

Saul of Tarsus was on his way to the next killing field when he experienced a vision of the resurrected Jesus. It didn't take Saul very long to refer to Jesus as Lord because he knew whoever He was, He was way bigger than he was. Jesus had Saul's attention. Jesus appointed Saul as a servant and a witness of what he had seen and what he would see. In essence, Jesus said, "I'm choosing you and you're going to go out and tell people what went down right here. You're going to tell them why you're doing what you're doing. I'm talking to you person-ally, Jack, are you listening?" Yeah, Saul was listening, and he set out right then and there as a servant of God and as Paul the Apostle.

Like Saul of Tarsus, I'm going forth to open the eyes of the nonbelievers, turn them from darkness to light, and turn them from the power of Satan to God. The spirit of the Evil One is working in everyone outside of Jesus. Those who live outside of Christ are prisoners of sin and have been taken captive by the Evil One. If you look at the playing field on earth, those under the control of the Evil One far outnumber the people of Jesus, and the gap is getting bigger and bigger every day.

What has changed between when Paul the Apostle lived in the first century and now? Nothing has changed whatsoever. We as believers are fighting the same battle he fought. We're fighting the same evil power he was fighting. We're dealing with the same human beings he dealt with. According to Ephesians 2, people outside of Christ are dead in their sin. The only thing that saves any of us is the grace of Jesus. Those of us who follow Christ are trying to share this message and deliver people from the power of Satan.

How are we going to win? Ephesians 6:10–20 provides us the battle plan:

Finally, be strong in the Lord and in his mighty power. Put on the full armor of God, so that you can take your stand against the devil's schemes. For our struggle is not against flesh and blood, but against the rulers, against the authorities, against the powers of this dark world and against the spiritual forces of evil in the heavenly realms. Therefore put on the full armor of God, so that when the day of evil comes, you may be able to stand your ground, and after you have done everything, to stand. Stand firm then, with the belt of truth buckled around your waist, with the breastplate of righteousness in place, and with your feet fitted with the readiness that comes from the gospel of peace. In addition to all this, take up the shield of faith, with which you can extinguish all the flaming arrows of the evil one. Take the helmet of salvation and the sword of the Spirit, which is the word of God.

And pray in the Spirit on all occasions with all kinds of prayers and requests. With this in mind, be alert and always keep on praying for all the Lord's people. Pray also for me, that whenever I speak, words may be given me so that I will fearlessly make known the mystery of the gospel, for which I am an ambassador in chains. Pray that I may declare it fearlessly, as I should.

Now, many Americans will think I'm speaking in some foreign language when I say we've got to be strong in the Lord and in His mighty power so we can take our stand against the devil's schemes. We need to put on the full armor of God. Say what? What's this nut talking about? From then until now, it's the same battle and same enemy. It's the same sins and same solution—Jesus. Humans were in the crosshairs of Satan then and still are today. Turn your back on Jesus, and you've got hell to pay. God loves you, and He proved that by sending Jesus to earth. But God will not be mocked.

I'm talking about war. But we're not at war with *people*; we're at war with the Evil One who *controls* those outside of Christ. As it says in the Scripture, "our struggle is not against flesh and blood." It's God versus Satan and good versus evil. Regardless of the depth of their sins, we still love the people outside of Jesus, and we're trying to set them free from Satan and sin. The Gospel of Jesus does that.

Hey, I'm a human being living on planet Earth and so are all of my neighbors in America. And some of those people are shredding our country to bits and pieces. But our struggles are against the powers of the dark world and against the spiritual forces of evil in the heavenly realms. Make no mistake: evil is here and it's organized. Satan and his mighty throng of evil demons that are with him gained control of the hearts and souls of men and women worldwide, and therein planet Earth is a big battlefield.

> **We're not at war with *people*; we're at war with the Evil One who *controls* those outside of Christ.**

What do we do? We go forth and we're armed. Not with

guns, but with the full armor of God. It's invisible, but it's real, and it provides rock-solid protection against the Evil One's onslaught. When the day of evil comes, we'll be able to stand our ground with armor God gives us.

It starts with the *Belt of Truth* buckled around our waist, and that truth is the death, burial, and resurrection of Jesus Christ. We'll be able to see through Satan's lies by holding them against the truth of the Bible.

Next, we'll put on the *Breastplate of Righteousness* because God—by His grace—has made us right with Him based on what He did through Jesus; our righteousness has nothing to do with what we do—nothing. When we accept the sacrificial death of Jesus Christ on the cross as our righteousness, and through our faith, God makes us righteous. We can't make ourselves righteous through our own good works. We're not good enough. The Breast-plate of Righteousness keeps our hearts strong and pure for God.

Our feet will be fitted with the readiness that comes from the *Gospel of Peace*. Only the gospel of Jesus can bring us all together. If you want peace and harmony in this country, or wherever you are on earth, only the gospel of Jesus can do it. Where there is no Jesus, evil reigns. The Gospel of Peace reminds us that it is by grace that souls are saved.

In addition, we'll take up the *Shield of Faith*, which can extinguish all the flaming arrows of the Evil One. He's alive and well and shoots doubt at us. By holding the Shield of Faith, we know our Father can be counted on.

Finally, we put on the *Helmet of Salvation* and the *Sword of the Spirit*, which is the weapon we fight with. The Helmet of Salvation protects our heads, where we know the truth of salvation sets us free. The Sword of the Spirit is the Bible, which is the Word of God.

When we're fully clothed in God's armor, we're ready to go forth and do battle against the dark forces of this world. We'll be equipped to teach others about Jesus and save those who are lost. Our cause is God's cause. It is right, it is just, and I for one will not relent, back up, or back off. I am all in for Jesus. Even though we're outnumbered, I like our chances. Are you with me?

13

---❖---

SIN

Fix No. 13: Repent and Ask God for Forgiveness

When A&E TV executives came to West Monroe, Louisiana, about three years ago and told us they wanted to produce a reality TV show about our family, they told me they were looking to make a show about family values. Having watched some of the disgusting filth we see in reality TV these days, I kind of scratched my head and had my doubts.

"You want to film a TV show about rednecks shooting ducks?" I asked them. "Do you actually think that will work?"

"Oh, we think it will work," they told me. "We're looking for a show about family values."

"Well, let me guess how this thing went down and then tell me if I'm correct," I told them. "You guys were probably sitting in your big boardroom in New York, and a bunch of you suits were tossing around ideas. A guy in the back of the room stood up and said, 'I know this is way out there, but is it possible to make a reality show about a functional American family?'

"'Functional family'?" another guy probably said. "'Now, Bob, that's a novel idea! But where would you find one on this earth, let alone in America?'"

I asked one of the A&E executives sitting in my living room, "Am I pretty close to how it went down?"

"Mr. Robertson, you're pretty close to how it went down," he said.

Well, *Duck Dynasty* made its debut in March 2012 and broke about every TV ratings record for reality TV over the past two years. To be honest, the show's popularity made me feel a little bit better about where America is headed because it's obvious that a large segment of our country was attracted to a close-knit family that loves God and loves one another. Of course, A&E's suits were happy, happy, happy because our ratings were through the roof, and they were generating millions and millions of dollars in advertising revenue.

Everything moved along pretty smoothly until December 2013, when *GQ* magazine published a cover story about *Duck Dynasty*. I didn't think much about it when I was told a reporter from *GQ* wanted to come to my house to interview us in October 2013. I really didn't care for it, but I agreed to do it because I was told it would be good publicity for our TV show. When the reporter showed up, I was sitting in my living room with three of my sons—Willie, Jase, and Jep—and my brother Silas, along with a public relations specialist from A&E TV.

The reporter, Drew Magary, introduced himself to me.

"Hey, what does *GQ* stand for?" I asked him.

The reporter started laughing because he thought I was joking. I wasn't, because I had never heard of the magazine.

"Are you serious?" he asked me. "*Gentleman's Quarterly.*"

"Yeah, I'm serious," I said. "Evidently, I don't run in the circle of gentlemen who read this particular magazine."

After a little bit of small talk, Magary asked Jase and Jep a couple of questions. They were sitting on one of the sofas in the room, and I learned after the interviews that the first questions out of the reporter's mouth were about my sons' sexual history. He asked Jep when he lost his virginity, and then he asked Jase if he really expected America to believe that he didn't have premarital sex with his wife, Missy, before they were married. I didn't even know he'd asked my boys those questions. If I had known that's how the interview started, I might have ended it right then. Jase was pretty upset about the guy's question and told him he wouldn't answer another one. So the guy made his way over to where I was sitting in my camouflage recliner.

The first question out of his mouth to me was: "Do you think homosexual behavior is a sin?"

Immediately, I began to question what kind of interview it was going to be. Well, he had asked a man who is a champion of family values whether he believed homosexuality is a sin, so

I quoted him a list of sins from the Bible from memory. Where else would one go to learn whether or not homosexuality is a sin? A dictionary? A medical textbook? A blogger on the Internet? I don't think so. As recently as October 4, 1982, the United States Congress proclaimed that the Bible is the Word of God, so I paraphrased scripture from Leviticus 18 and then 1 Corinthians 6, which is where Paul the Apostle spoke from God and wrote a list of sins, which includes homosexuality. When Paul wrote 1 Corinthians 6, God was speaking through him, according to 2 Peter 1:20–21: *"Above all, you must understand that no prophecy of Scripture came about by the prophet's own interpretation of things. For prophecy never had its origin in the human will, but prophets, though human, spoke from God as they were carried along by the Holy Spirit."* Also, 2 Timothy 3:16 says, *"All Scripture is God-breathed and is useful for teaching, rebuking, correcting and training in righteousness."*

The scripture I quoted to the *GQ* reporter was written by Paul and is what God said, so I believe it to be true. So when the reporter asked me if I believed homosexuality is a sin, I quoted Scripture, specifically, 1 Corinthians 6:9–10, which says: *"Or do you not know that wrongdoers will not inherit the kingdom of God? Do not be deceived: Neither the sexually immoral nor idolaters nor adulterers nor men who have sex with men nor thieves nor the greedy nor drunkards nor slanderers nor swindlers will inherit the kingdom of God."*

Those are the words of Paul the Apostle, who was personally chosen by Jesus Christ to write most of the New Testament. They are God's words. In my opinion, the really sad part about the flap from the *GQ* interview is that most of the mainstream media in America didn't even know I was quoting from the Bible. Apparently, they believed I was just running my mouth. Believe the Scripture or don't believe it—it is what Paul wrote, it is what God told him to write, and it is what I quoted to the reporter. What happened next is for all of you to digest and then decide if you believe the words or not.

Here's my question: If you have a man who is part of a TV show about family values and who is a champion of family values, how do you expect him to respond to a question about sin? If you look at the list of sins I paraphrased for the dude, including sexual immorality, adultery, theft, greed, drunkenness, homosexuality, and swindling, what kind of values do you suppose the individuals who participate in those sins would have? *Not* godly ones. But when A&E asked for family values, what the executives were actually asking for was godliness, because the best family values come about when God is involved. We're godly people with family values.

> Believe the Scripture or don't believe it—it is what Paul wrote, it is what God told him to write, and it is what I quoted to the reporter.

Just after quoting the Scripture to the reporter, I gave him an opinion of mine based on my logic as a heterosexual male. I called a vagina a vagina and an anus an anus, which is how any dictionary or medical textbook refers to those particular parts of the human anatomy. I guess I might have referred to the vagina as the "canal between the vulva and the uterus" and the anus as the "opening at the end of the alimentary canal." I'm not sure how many of *GQ*'s readers would have known what I was talking about, but I didn't think the words I used were crude. I called each body part exactly what it was. Hey, news flash: I'm a heterosexual man. I prefer the vagina—get it?

Obviously, a certain segment of the population was offended by my quotes. But you have to understand that our family values are the fruit of the Holy Spirit, which is living inside us. That fruit is love, joy, peace, patience, kindness, goodness, faithfulness, gentleness, and self-control (Galatians 5:22–23). This list of family values comes straight from the Holy Spirit of God. When people watch *Duck Dynasty*, they see those values among our family. Stack that list up against the other list: sexual immorality, idolatry, adultery, thievery, drunkenness, and greed. It's not a match.

Was I mad about being put on indefinite hiatus? No, I was sad about it. I wasn't mad then, and I'm still not mad today. The people who were upset about what I said blamed me, but I only quoted the Apostle Paul. If they want to be mad at someone, blame Paul, who only wrote what God told him to write. My critics would in fact be blaming God, because all scripture is God-breathed. The sins are the same today as when the scripture was written more than two thousand years ago in about 50 AD. It's a plain, succinct Bible passage that lists a series of behaviors that are sins, with eternal judgment being the punishment for those sins. In Galatians 5:19–21, Paul wrote another list of sins: *"The acts of the flesh are obvious: sexual immorality, impurity and debauchery; idolatry and witchcraft; hatred, discord, jealousy, fits of rage, selfish ambition, dissensions, factions and envy; drunkenness, orgies, and the like. I warn you, as I did before, that those who live like this will not inherit the kingdom of God."* Paul said the same thing to the Galatians that he said to the Corinthians, but he added a few more sins to the list for the Galatians.

One thing to remember is that homosexuality is one of several in the list of sins. It isn't elevated above any of the other sins. I am not a homophobe; I only fear for sinners' souls. And those sinners include people who are greedy, who are filled with hatred or given to fits of rage, drunkenness, and the like. I love everyone even if they dislike me. I never pronounce judgment on anyone—ever. I only give them the Good News and move on down the road. I told the reporter that the Apostle Paul said sinners wouldn't inherit the kingdom of God. On my own, I wouldn't have told him even that because I'm not an inspired man. If the *GQ* reporter had asked me if I believed drunkenness was a sin, I would have read him the same scripture. If he had asked me about greed, envy, rage, self-ambition, or hatred, I would have given him the same list. I wouldn't have even thought about homosexuality if he hadn't asked me about it. I didn't make homosexual behavior a target; he asked me about it. In hindsight, it's amazing that none of the people who are fornicating and committing heterosexual immorality ever called me to complain. None of the greedy or envious people ever called me to tell me I was wrong. None of the thieves or drunkards sent me letters of complaint. As late-night TV host Jay Leno joked one night, I actually thought some politicians from Congress might call me because I talked about slanderers and swindlers. Much to my surprise, not one of them ever contacted me.

John 3:16 tells us: *"For God so loved the world that he gave his one and only Son, that whoever believes in him shall not perish but have eternal life."* Now, there is the crux of the matter. God loved the world so much that He sent Jesus to save us and whoever believes in Him won't perish. The next verse is the one too many of us forget: *"For God did not send his Son into the world to condemn the world, but to save the world through him"* (John 3:17). Jesus told us that He wasn't sent to the world to condemn it. Therefore, we can't look at any group of people and condemn them. We can only give them the Good News, love them, and pray for them. I'll leave judgment up to the Almighty.

> If the *GQ* reporter had asked me if I believed drunkenness was a sin, I would have read him the same scripture.

What the *GQ* reporter left out of the story and what a lot of people seemed to gloss over was that after Paul gave the Corinthians the list of sins, he finished with the following scripture: *"And that is what some of you were. But you were washed, you were sanctified, you were justified in the name of the Lord*

Jesus Christ and by the Spirit of God" (1 Corinthians 6:11). Paul was trying to encourage them and described how they used to behave. But the Good News—and this is what much of America missed—is that God erased their sins and forgave them. Paul was warning them not to go back to their former lives.

The most important thing I want everyone to realize is that the scripture in 1 Corinthians 6:11 is encouraging and is far from hateful in any way. Paul was giving the Corinthians an escape hatch to get out from under their sin. It was a great thing to tell someone. What a great thing for God to do back then and what a great thing He can do in America today. The sins in the list Paul sent to the Corinthians were common then, and they're common in America today. They were forgiven then, and we can be forgiven now. The problem comes when we won't acknowledge our sins and turn from them. Instead of people repenting of their sins and turning to God, they were mad at me; instead of acknowledging that they were sinners, according to what Paul the Apostle wrote in the Bible, they were angry at me. Instead, I was simply answering his question and giving him a way out of the current predicament he's in today.

Because I love you, I must give you some final words of advice. I understand the health risks of any immoral conduct, heterosexual or homosexual. I also talked with medical professionals after I did my research. I was stunned and saddened by the sheer volume of the various sexually transmitted diseases that accompany immoral conduct. It is far more dangerous to your physical health than I originally thought.

Some people attacked me when I told the *GQ* reporter that sexual immorality of any kind is a sin. I was telling him the truth, according to the Bible! I told the truth then, and I'm telling the truth now. Look, I used to be an immoral man. I came out of the sixties. I used to stand in their shoes. I used to be on their side. I used to rail, gripe, moan, and attack what I called the "thumpers." Most of the time, though, I only tried to stay away from the godly. I hated people like me back then, like some of the people hate me now! My defense for my sins was exactly the defense many of them are now using against me. I look back at my wild days and remember my rants, in which I called them "those goody-goody hypocrites." How dare they try to tell me how to run my life! I hated them. I hated the sight of them, with their Bibles under their arms while they delivered hellfire-and-brimstone sermons.

But you know something? Way down deep inside me, I knew that it wasn't them who had a problem. It was me who had a problem—a big one—and I finally got it when I realized sin was living in me. It was the Evil One who had ensnared me and held me fast. It was not the fault of the messengers who tried to get me to change from my evil ways. My hatred was toward God Himself. He was the one I was rebelling against. My generation reached its formative years during what they called the "sexual revolution." Simply put, it was the "sinful revolution."

Do you know how I knew I was the problem and not God? My conscience told me. I used to be just like many of the sinners are now—on the wrong side but too hateful and prideful to admit it. My run with the wicked lasted from high school until a few years after I finished college. I am ashamed of it now, especially all those sins. But at the time I was involved in it, I wasn't ashamed of anything! I was the hater then! Hey, do you know why I speak out against sin? I'm saying these things because I am now a minister of reconciliation. God has sent me and others to try to reconcile the lost to Him through Jesus, and He has given us the message of reconciliation, namely, the death of Jesus, His burial, and His resurrection for any who are without Him.

It is the truth that sets us free from the sins we have committed over the years. I'm saying these things because, along with other believers, I represent Jesus here on earth—that's what a follower of Christ is called to. Consider me an ambassador for Jesus. He loves sinners and so do I. In this case, God is making His appeal

> Do you know how I knew I was the problem and not God? My conscience told me.

through me, and He also makes His appeal through many others like me. We are the "repentant" ones. We've been there, done that, and seen the error of our ways. When we heard the message we believed it, repented, and were born again in Christ Jesus. I am a "new creation" in Christ; He did everything for me, and He has done everything for you.

Think about it: if I did not love lost people, why would I spend the time or effort to say these things? Are they mad at me because I love them? I believe the Evil One is behind that logic. My only regret is that I did not turn to God earlier in my life. It would have saved Miss Kay a lot of pain, along with my young sons and family members back then. But you know something? It's never too late to begin the journey with God.

You're not kidding this ol' dude. I didn't have peace of mind before I found Jesus. None! I have it now, though. Why? I was wrong back then—dead wrong—but I am right about Jesus, and if you are not reconciled to God, I implore you to be reconciled! You will find a peace that surpasses understanding, and the blood of Jesus is more than sufficient to remove every last sin you have ever committed—sexual or otherwise. Go ahead and rip into me if you like. I will still love you in spite of it. Remember this one thing: you know the way out of your sinful dilemma because God has appointed me to tell you, and I have done so. I have done my job on your behalf, and I will continue to pray for you.

I do not fear sinners at all. In fact, we're *all* sinners. But some of us sinners have placed our faith in Christ and been saved by His blood. I love those outside of Christ, and my love is too strong for me to be afraid of them. The flap over the *GQ* interview didn't bother me one bit, and I didn't lose any sleep over it. My prayer is that everyone in America who needs to repent will turn from their sins and learn to love. All we can do is share the Good News with others, telling them Jesus came to earth more than two thousand years ago to save us from our sin. The nonbelievers count time by Jesus, just as we do. We tell them He died for our sins, which are many, and that three days after His death, He rose from the dead to guarantee that we can have our sins removed and get out from under the yoke of Satan. It is a daunting task to alert others about Jesus, but I am up to the task, even if some people hate me for it. You see, folks, my love for the ones caught up in their evil ideologies is not contingent upon how they feel about me. It is not me they have a problem with—it is Jesus—and I simply represent Him. I pray they have a change of heart and repent their sins.

Which list are you in? Where do you stand before God? What list do you practice? You have seen the two lists. One includes love, joy, peace, patience, kindness, goodness, faithfulness, gentleness, and self-control; the other includes sexual immorality, idolatry, adultery, homosexuality, thievery, greed, drunkenness, slander, and swindling. Boy, it is easy to find out who someone really is if you watch their actions. You can usually tell by what comes out of our mouths and what we do after dark. Just read the two lists and we can probably identify who we really are. One list guarantees eternal death and the other list has no laws against anything on it. I would encourage you to think about those things. I am not your judge. There is a judge, but it's not me. I judge no person and condemn no one. I only want America's culture to change for the better. I'm quoting you the sins and telling you what God did through Jesus to forgive you. You can take it or leave it; it's your call. I can't make the call for you. But remember this: whichever way you decide to go, I'll love you anyway.

14

⸻◦◉◦⸻

DEATH

Fix No. 14: Prepare for the Recall

During nearly seven decades on this earth, one of the things that has really struck me is the temporary nature of all living things. As I told you earlier, American men can expect to live about seventy-six years, maybe a few more if we're lucky and a lot less if we're not so fortunate. Women can expect to live a little longer than men, and the healthiest among us might even live to be about ninety years old or older.

Hey, we should be counting our blessings. If you look at some of the species in the animal kingdom, they have much shorter life spans than humans. Rabbits live for an average of only nine years (and reproduce like, well, rabbits while they're here), and hamsters and guinea pigs live about four years. Drag-onflies, which hover over ponds and rivers like miniature helicopters during the summertime, only survive for an average of about two months. A dragonfly might remain in its nymph state for four years, waiting for the perfect time to begin its life, only to stay on earth for around sixty days or so. A mayfly, which is one of the main sources of food for fish on a river, might live less than twenty-four hours. Naiads, the larval form of mayflies, live up to a year in the water before becoming adults. After mayflies wait so long to become full-fledged insects, they might live for only a few minutes, or a few days at most.

After reading and studying the Bible over and over again during the last four decades, I'm convinced that God originally created humans to live for hundreds of years. I think He did it to populate the earth. It took humanity a long time to get the population going, especially after God wiped out all but eight humans with the Great Flood, so He programmed them to live a lot longer than we do now. It probably helped that they didn't have fast-food restaurants and other junk food around to pollute their bodies!

You might have heard the saying "He's as old as Methuselah." The oldest man who ever lived is believed to be Methuselah, who was linked to Adam and Noah and lived to be 969 years old. God introduces us to him in Genesis 5:21–27:

When Enoch had lived 65 years, he became the father of Methuselah. After he became the father of Methuselah, Enoch walked faithfully with God 300 years and had other sons and daughters. Altogether, Enoch lived a total of 365 years. Enoch walked faithfully with God; then he was no more, because God took him away.

When Methuselah had lived 187 years, he became the father of Lamech. After he became the father of Lamech, Methuselah lived 782 years and had other sons and daughters. Altogether, Methuselah lived a total of 969 years, and then he died.

The United Nations estimates that there were about three hundred million people living on earth when God sent Jesus to live among us. It took one thousand years for the population to increase to three hundred ten million and then another two hundred and fifty years for it to reach four hundred million in 1250 AD. You have to remember that they didn't have antibiotics like penicillin around back then, and people around the world dropped like flies when they became sick. If you had some kind of contagion like the plague going around, oh my goodness, it really put a dent in the world's population. That's one of the reasons the world's population kind of flatlined for so long.

It took about sixteen hundred years for the world's population to double to six hundred million in 1600 AD. It didn't reach one billion until 1804. Then, in the span of only two hundred years, the population increased more than six times over to more than six billion in 2000. In the twentieth century alone, the world's population increased from 1.65 billion to six billion.

That's a lot of procreating! The UN estimates the world's population will reach ten billion people by the year 2200. People are still dying across the world, obviously, but a lot more people are being born every year. Plus, humans are living a lot longer. The life expectancy of a human has increased by twenty years since 1950, and the UN predicts it will increase to seventy-six years across the world by 2050.

Hey, folks, we're running out of real estate on planet Earth! Now you know why scientists are so interested in other planets like Mars and Saturn. They're looking for somewhere else for everyone to live. How in the world are we going to feed ten billion people in less than two hundred years from now? I guess that's one of the reasons birth control, including abortion, is sanctioned by so many governments nowadays. Countries all over the world are looking for every kind of way known to man to curtail Earth's population.

But here's what the save-the-planet groups and census counters forget: the Bible tells us that one day Earth will be discarded like a worn-out dishcloth. The Scripture tells us it will get paper-thin and wear out, so let's be realistic about saving the planet.

Hey, folks, we're running out of real estate on planet Earth!

Conserving fossil fuels is a hot political issue in America, and we're aggressively searching for other forms of energy, like wind, solar, and nuclear. Scientists say there's no way fossil fuels will sustain us, not with more than seven billion people consuming them around the world. You can only punch and drill so many holes in the earth, so they're looking for other ways to fuel our automobiles, heat and power our homes, and cook our food.

I'm telling you right now that it's an exercise in futility. Of course we must be good stewards of the earth God gave us and care for and respect it the best we can, but we have to remember that God didn't design our planet to last for eternity. *"In the past God spoke to our ancestors through the prophets at many times and in various ways, but in these last days he has spoken to us by his Son, whom he appointed heir of all things, and through whom also he made the universe"* (Hebrews 1:1–2). The Hebrews writer wrote that scripture in about 65 AD, and he was already referring to the "last days." It has been Earth's final days ever since Jesus came here. Up until then, things were rocking along and God was working with His people "at many times and in various ways."

Now it's 2014. How many more dramatic things are going to happen, biblically speaking? There's only one last event—Jesus' return—because everything else has already occurred. God created the cosmos and then drowned everyone on Earth. After the Great Flood, God gave humans the Law of Moses, putting everyone under a code a couple of thousand years before Jesus was born. Then God sent us Jesus, His only Son, and He was crucified and then rose from the dead. Jesus has already gone back to heaven, so what's the only thing left?

The only thing left, according to the Bible, is the return of Jesus. Then Earth and everything on it will be destroyed. Men won't destroy it; God says He's going to destroy it this time. Read the scripture again. When the Hebrews writer says, *"but in these last days he has spoken to us by his Son,"* that's the reason we need to get behind Jesus. Jesus is the heir of everything, and He's our only escape hatch off Earth. He's the radiance of God's glory and is the exact representation of His being. He sustains all things by His powerful Word. After He provided us with purification from sin, He sat down at the right hand of the Majesty in heaven. He went back to where He came from.

When is Jesus coming back? What's the holdup? We don't know when Jesus is coming. Second Peter 3:4 says: *"They will say, 'Where is this "coming" he promised? Ever since our ancestors died, everything goes on as it has since the beginning of creation.'"* The unbelievers forget that long ago, according to God's Word, the earth was formed out of water—and then He destroyed it with water. They forget that God has already drowned mankind once before. The present heavens and earth are reserved for fire. He did it with water the first time, with fire being reserved for the Day of Judgment. Trust me, we're not going to destroy Earth—He is. Of course we can and should be good stewards of the earth while we're on it, but we can't "save" it. It's meant to come to an end. I'm with God, and I don't want anyone to perish, as Peter says in 2 Peter 3:9: *"The Lord is not slow in keeping his promise, as some understand slowness. Instead he is patient with you, not wanting anyone to perish, but everyone to come to repentance."* That's my desire, too. I want everyone to come to repentance. My desire is to help others out. That's why I'm telling everyone to turn from their sins and accept Jesus Christ as their Lord and Savior.

Now, we've heard plenty of predictions about the end of the world throughout the history of mankind. Nostradamus predicted the world would end in 3797 AD. Remember the Y2K phenomenon, when our calendars turned to January 1, 2000? People around the world predicted doomsday scenarios of the rapture, the war of Armageddon, the second coming of Jesus, and the appearance of the antichrist. But other than a few computers shutting down, nothing really happened. Some scholars believed that the Mayans, who lived in Central America from about 1500 BC to 1519 AD, carved into their calendars that the world would end on December 21, 2012, but that day came and went without anything happening. From Branch Davidian leader David Koresh to a woman in Conyers, Georgia, who claimed to see images of Mary and Jesus, people all over the world have predicted the end of Earth. Obviously, none of it ever came true.

We have to remember that no one knows when Jesus is coming back. *"But the day of the Lord will come like a thief"* (2 Peter 3:10). Hey, so much for making a prediction about when Earth will end. He is going to come back like a thief, and no one knows when a thief is going to rob you, right? God is an eternal being and time doesn't pass for Him, not one second. Time only goes by for us. He's outside of time and is omniscient (all-knowing), omnipotent (all-powerful), and omnipresent (present everywhere). He's a spirit and one super-powerful being.

When Jesus returns, here's what's going to happen, according to 2 Peter 3:10–13:

The heavens will disappear with a roar; the elements will be destroyed by fire, and the earth and everything done in it will be laid bare.

Since everything will be destroyed in this way, what kind of people ought you to be? You ought to live holy and godly lives as you look forward to the day of God and speed its coming. That day will bring about the destruction of the heavens by fire, and the elements will melt in the heat. But in keeping with his promise we are looking forward to a new heaven and a new earth, where righteousness dwells.

Now, use your own judgment about what was just said there. I have an idea: God is going to resurrect and make another Earth, one in which we'll have eternity with God. Simply put, God created it all, created us, waited, and no time has passed for Him. Then He is going to step back in and destroy it all. But the ones who put their faith in Jesus will live eternally like Him, and we'll get a new heaven and a new Earth. God, in His love and mercy, has made human beings so they can live eternally like Him, instead of being swept away forever and ever.

Being cast to hell is missing the opportunity to live eternally. Whether you believe that hell is an actual burning fire or that the descriptions of hell in the Scripture are metaphors, the bottom line is that you can live forever with God, or you can be separated from him for eternity.

Because of my faith, I'm not one who cries at funerals and mourns a loved one's death. Sure, I hate that they're not here on earth with me anymore, but I know one day soon we'll be together again with Jesus. I believe Jesus died and rose again, so I believe God will bring with Jesus those who have fallen asleep in Him. I don't think He'll take our bodies from the cemetery. When Jesus makes His final return, He'll bring back our souls and spirits, whether our earthly bodies were laid to rest one thousand years ago or ten years ago. Our souls and spirits will be reunited with a glorified body, an eternal body. I don't think there's any doubt about it—we'll have some kind of body. That's why Jesus came back from the dead bodily. His disciples touched Him and fed Him fish. Forty days after His resurrection, Jesus ascended from the earth and returned to the heavens. His eleven disciples were looking in the sky, saying, "Good grief. That's a glimpse of the body we're going to get when Jesus returns." That is the story the Bible tells us, and I personally think it's a little too wild for humans to dream up.

When we physically die on

> You can live forever and be conscious with God, or you can go back to the oblivious state and not exist anymore.

earth, our heart stops beating and our loved ones bury our bodies in a cemetery or cremate us. We leave our bodies behind, but we're still alive in soul and spirit. No time will pass as we wait for Jesus to return.

A few years ago, I underwent surgery to have a kidney stone removed. The kidney stone was pretty painful, so I finally relented and had it surgically removed. I usually have a pretty good pain threshold, but that sucker was painful.

As I was lying on the operating table, the doctors gave me anesthesia and I closed my eyes. The next thing I knew, I was waking up. "How long did that take?" I asked the doctor.

"About an hour," he told me.

"Now I understand the resurrection," I said.

The doctor looked at me and then turned to a nurse.

"He's hallucinating," he said.

"I'm not hallucinating," I told him. "I lost that hour because I was dead asleep. Look, it could have been ten hours. It would have been the same thing. I would have closed my eyes and then woken up. I would have still been dead asleep. It wouldn't have made any difference because no time was passing for me."

Honestly, it might have been one thousand years, no difference. You close your eyes and then open them. That's resurrection time. No one is sitting in their grave, twiddling their thumbs, waiting for the second coming of Jesus. They're dead asleep, but their soul is alive and waiting. When is Jesus coming? I don't know and neither does anyone else. Let's look at 2 Peter 3 one more time. It tells us never to forget one thing: *"With the Lord a day is like a thousand years, and a thousand years are like a day. The Lord is not slow in keeping his promise, as some understand slowness. Instead he is patient with you, not wanting anyone to perish, but everyone to come to repentance"* (verses 8–9). Jesus is waiting, and He wants more of us to turn from our sins and repent. He doesn't want anyone to perish.

As I think about the second coming of Jesus, I'm reminded of the recall notices I find in my mailbox from time to time. It seems like automobile manufacturers are recalling their vehicles more than ever before because of safety concerns. If we're spending an arm and leg to purchase a new car or truck, you would think the automobile companies would build them safe the first time. In 2013 alone, auto manufacturers recalled twenty-two million cars and trucks in the United States. Jesus' return is like a recall on mankind. We don't know when it's coming, but don't believe that it won't happen. Eventually, we're all going to have to stand before God and give an account of our lives. And make no mistake about it: He's going to recall us because we're broken. We're all sinners, but it's not too late to turn from our sins and come to Christ Jesus.

You close your eyes and then open them. That's resurrection time.

15

◈

GOOD NEWS

Fix No. 15: Embrace Jesus Christ

In the last two chapters, we've talked about the bad news: sin and death. We can't really understand how good the Good News is until we understand how bad off we are without it. But there is a way out of our sad predicament. Are you ready for it? Here it is: *"Here is a trustworthy saying that deserves full acceptance: Christ Jesus came into the world to save sinners"* (1 Timothy 1:15).

If this statement isn't true, then you can pretty much disregard everything I've written in this book.

But I'm going to warn you: we wouldn't be better off for it. We'd be far worse off, because if Jesus didn't die to save us, then we have six-foot holes waiting for us and that will be the end of us. However, if the statement is true—and I certainly believe that it is—then we have hope beyond the grave. If Jesus didn't die for us, then we all lose, and the grave ends it. If He did, then some of us will win, and sadly, the people who don't place their faith in Him will lose.

After reading this book—especially the last two chapters—I hope I've helped you reach the conclusion that there are two problems we can't fix. We can't solve them for ourselves, the government can't solve them, and medical technology can't solve them.

The first problem is sin, and it's what's plaguing the world today. When we come from our mothers we don't yet have a sense of right and wrong. But when we reach a certain age and know right from wrong, we all violate what we know to be right (see Romans 2:15). Romans 1:20 says that through His creation, God has made Himself known

> **If Jesus didn't die to save us, then we have six-foot holes waiting for us and that will be the end of us.**

to everyone: *"For since the creation of the world God's invisible qualities—his eternal power and divine nature—have been clearly seen, being understood from what has been made, so that people are without excuse."* When we're old enough, we violate whatever law we know in some form or fashion. In fact, most of us violate it over and over again. Once we commit the first violation, we die spiritually in the eyes of God. All we have to do is never violate what we know to be right, and we'll have nothing to worry about. Well, since we're all humans, we all sin and none of us are perfect. So the bad news is: sin is a real problem.

But sin isn't our only problem. After we've sinned, we walk around the rest of our lives waiting on *physical death*. The first problem is spiritual death, and then physical death comes along. But if we've accepted Jesus Christ as our Lord and Savior, our problems are solved. Jesus Christ is the solution to sin and death. He is the one we count time by—ever since He came to this earth 2,014 years ago. He is the one who was, in fact, God in flesh. God was born to a human mother, just like we were. The difference between Jesus and us is that He never violated the law. God, in His kindness and love for us, chose to fix our sin and death problems—which would have separated us from Him for eternity—by allowing Jesus to take our punishment on Himself and become the perfect sacrifice.

God decided He would make us perfect, but we have to come to Him through Jesus to be viewed as perfect. When we place our trust in Jesus, God doesn't count our sins against us. *"Blessed is the one whose transgressions are forgiven, whose sins are covered. Blessed is the one whose sin the Lord does not count against them and in whose spirit is no deceit"* (Psalm 32:1–2). God provided forgiveness of our sins through Jesus by sending Him to Earth and allowing human beings to take His life. Now, a lot of people were crucified in the first century. But Jesus was God in the human body and was crucified for the sins of the world. The price paid by God to remove your sin and mine was the blood of a holy, perfect God who was in a human body. Jesus died so our sins would be removed.

Jesus solved our first problem—sin—by dying on the cross. And He's also the solution to our second problem—physical death. In the first century they did the same thing with their deceased that we do in the twenty-first century. They buried them. They buried Jesus, and then three days later, our second problem was solved when Jesus came forth from the grave alive. He came out of the grave bodily and He was alive. They thought He was a ghost, which makes sense to me. So He had them touch Him, feel Him with their hands, and He told them, *"A ghost does not have flesh and bones, as you see I have"* (Luke 24:39). A dead body went into the tomb, and then that body stood back up on earth. When I first read what happened to Jesus, it opened my eyes. The story convinced me that if there was ever any way to escape the grave, the escape route was right there—Jesus of Galilee. Jesus removed our sin and was raised from the dead. He convinced Constantine of it back in about the fourth century, and He convinced me of it about two thousand years later.

It's our way out of here; I'm wholly convinced of it. The Good News is that all you have to do is believe, and it's free of charge. It's the grace of God personified in the death, burial, and resurrection of Jesus. It is the gospel. It won't cost you anything. The only thing you have to do is believe it, turn from whatever sins you have, and change your mind. You want change and hope? Change your mind because of Jesus and put your hope in His resurrection from the dead—that's the greatest hope anybody can have. The gospel and the grace of God are the source of change and hope—and they're about the only free things you're ever going to find while you're living on planet Earth.

Escaping your grave isn't hard. Repent of your sins and confess Jesus as Lord. Then follow through by having somebody take you to a pond, creek, or pothole and baptize you. The reason you do this is the one Who died and was buried and raised from the dead said, *"All authority in heaven and on earth has been given to me. Therefore go make disciples of all nations, baptizing them in the name of the Father and of the Son and of the Holy Spirit"* (Matthew 28:18–19). Those were His marching orders—some of His last words after His resurrection and before He ascended back

> The gospel and the grace of God are about the only free things you're ever going to find while you're living on planet Earth.

to heaven. Jesus' disciples did exactly what He instructed them to do. More than two thousand years later, as a follower of Jesus, I too am doing what He said to do. I'm doing the exact same thing. You can research all of it. The gospel is the same, Jesus is the same, and the response is the same. I'm not saying anything that you can't document, read, and verify on your own by simply picking up a Bible and reading it. I strongly suggest you do so.

Jesus told us to go forth and tell people the Good News, and that's what I'm doing. I condemn no one, and you don't have to judge anybody. Just go forth and tell people about Jesus. The power to save people is in the *story*. Just tell the story. I say with the Apostle Paul: *"I am not ashamed of the gospel, because it is the power of God that brings salvation to everyone who believes"* (Romans 1:16). The gospel will change people's hearts and lives, and others need to hear the Good News from our lips to their ears. I'm convinced of the power of the gospel to change.

You wouldn't believe how many people come to White's Ferry Road Church in West Monroe, Louisiana (where we attend), because of the popularity of *Duck Dynasty*. People drive in from all over the country to worship with us. They'll attend my Sunday school classes, and many of them will ask to be baptized in our church. Shortly after the flap over my interview with *GQ* magazine went viral, two people came to our church and told me they were upset about the way the media and other groups were portraying me.

My son Jase had baptized one of the men in the river many years earlier, but he had fallen away from God. We hadn't seen him in many years. The guy told me he was sitting in a bar, drinking heavily and snorting cocaine every thirty minutes, when he saw my picture on TV. He said he became enraged when he learned that people were giving me a hard time for reading a list of sins from the Bible. When he started yelling, other patrons in the bar scolded him. "How are you going to defend him?" someone in the bar asked him. "You're the sorriest guy around here." Those words convicted him. The man told me he was a drunkard, an adulterer, and sexually immoral.

He came to me and wept like a baby. He repented and renewed his faith.

"The only thing I can tell you is what you already know," I told him.

"Did you ever think I'd come back?" he asked me.

I told him we always loved him. As it says in Second Peter 2:20–22,

> *If they have escaped the corruption of the world by knowing our Lord and Savior Jesus Christ and are again entangled in it and are overcome, they are worse off at the end than they were in the beginning. It would have been better for them not to have known the way of righteousness, than to have known it and then to turn their backs on the sacred command that was passed on to them. Of them the proverbs are true: "A dog returns to its vomit," and "A sow that is washed returns to her wallowing in the mud."*

Knowledge, especially full knowledge, without obedience is exceedingly dangerous! But when the fallen return, we love them like we did before. It's like when we accepted my sons Alan and Jep after they strayed from their Christian paths. They were like the prodigal son returning home.

When the fallen return, we love them like we did before.

The second man had never known anything about Jesus. He was a heart surgeon and was vacationing with his family in Colorado when he saw me on the news. The man told me he feared he was becoming one of those doctors who thought he could play God, and his marriage was crumbling because of fighting, feuding, and infidelity. After the man saw me on TV, he told his family that their vacation was over. He and his wife attended my Sunday school class the following weekend. His wife was baptized at church that day, and the doctor was baptized in the Ouachita River next to our house a few weeks later in the middle of an ice storm. The water was so cold we had to put him in a wet suit so he wouldn't freeze. Now the doctor is sharing the Good News with others and trying to make amends for his past transgressions. Ironically, they owe their souls and salvation to what happened to me because of the *GQ* flap. As long as we saved one person's soul, the grief was worth it for me.

It warms my heart to see so many people affected by my family's story. We share the Good News with everyone, but not everyone receives it, which is fine. I worry about their souls, but I understand that we are in spiritual warfare, and not everyone will see the light. Who would have ever thought that Hollywood, through a reality TV show, would be financing the gospel being preached all over the United States and world? If someone had told me that Hollywood would be paying for me to go all over the country and preach the Good News, I would have told them they were off their rocker. It's almost like divine intervention is involved;

> Ironically, they owe their souls to what happened to me because of the *GQ* flap. As long as we saved one person's soul, the grief was worth it for me.

at least that's the way I'm leaning. I mean, the odds of it happening from this raggedy bunch of rednecks on the river makes you think there has to be a greater power working behind the scenes. That helps my faith in God.

Here's the deal, America: None of us is getting out of here alive—except through Jesus. He is the way, the truth, the life— He is the resurrection. There's no escape without going through Him. Hey, all you numbskulls, do you have a better idea for your own life? Do you have a better idea for fixing this rotten culture and sea of depravity we now find ourselves swimming in? Repent and live your life for Jesus. Turn your life around, turn your streets around, turn your cities around, turn your states around, turn this messed-up country around, and turn your world around. Look at yourself and look at everyone around us. Are you coming or not? Just remember this—even if you hate me, I love you anyway. So does God!

Are you contemplating believing that Jesus died for you and was raised from the dead? If you believe this message, then turn your sinful life around and confess with your mouth, "Jesus is my Lord." Then follow through by having someone baptize you in water. Then God will seal the deal by giving you His Spirit to live inside you. He'll help you to find love, joy, peace, patience, goodness, faithfulness, gentleness, and self-control. How could you possibly want anything more? The body that God will raise up will be "imperishable"(1 Corinthians 15:42). It won't be like the body we now have, which is very perishable. You see, when

Jesus said, *"You will know the truth, and the truth will set you free"* (John 8:32), the "truth" he was speaking about was His death, His burial, and His resurrection, which sets you free from law, sin, Satan, and even the guilt of your sin. Believe it or not, it even sets you free from the graves where you're surely going. That is freedom indeed. I can't figure out why everyone doesn't embrace Jesus! Why did God do these things through Jesus? He loves you. And because He loves me, I love you, too.

It doesn't matter how bad you think your sins are—you can be forgiven for all of them. I'm telling you the truth. It is time for all of America to repent and turn back to the Lord, and we had better do it now before it's too late for our beloved nation. Can you do that? Love God and love your neighbor. It's as simple as that. I'm doing it—not perfectly, but I'm doing it—and I'm not the only one. There are a lot more people doing it too, but not nearly enough. America, we need to get back to the gospel of Jesus as quickly as we can. If we do, we'll live happily, happily, happily ever after.

ACKNOWLEDGMENTS

To the crew at Howard Books and Simon & Schuster, y'all really know how to put together and sell books!

To Schlabach, for such a quiet man, you really know how to retell a story!

To Stephenson, for your brain power and meticulous attention to the details of our Creator!

To my family, you are my legacy that will carry forward these truths to the future!

To my forever family at WFR and the men I shepherd with there, you keep me grounded and engaged in the work of our Savior!

To the millions of people who rallied to my defense when I was being disparaged, I appreciate you and challenge you to be vigilant during these days of evil!

To my God, You rescued me from sin and depravity with grace and forgiveness with the gift of Your Son and You supplied me with power and the courage to never back away from truth with the gift of Your Spirit. Everything I do, I do for Your glory!